MOVING APPLICATIONS TO THE CLOUD

Moving Applications to the Cloud

on the Microsoft® Windows Azure™ Platform

Authors
   Dominic Betts
   Scott Densmore
   Ryan Dunn
   Masashi Narumoto
   Eugenio Pace
   Matias Woloski

ISBN: 9780735649675

Contents

Foreword

Millions of people are using cloud services from Microsoft; as a company, we're all in! And as someone who has been involved with Windows Azure since the beginning, it's gratifying to see this work come to fruition. For customers still exploring what the cloud means for them, this first Windows Azure architecture guide from the Microsoft patterns & practices team will answer many of the questions they may have. Microsoft is serious about cloud computing, and this guide is one of many investments that Microsoft is making to ensure that its customers are successful as they begin developing new applications or migrating existing applications to the cloud.

Developers familiar with .NET and the rest of the Microsoft platform will be able to use their existing skills to quickly build or move existing applications to the cloud and use the power of the cloud to scale to millions of users and reach everyone in the world. Yet, Windows Azure is an open platform that works well with other technology stacks and application frameworks, providing customers with the choice and flexibility to move as much or as little business to the cloud as they want and without needing to start over.

This guide is a great starting point for those who want to embark on this journey using a pragmatic, scenario-based approach.

Sincerely,
Amitabh Srivastava
Senior Vice President, Windows Azure

Foreword

Microsoft's recent release of the Windows Azure platform, an operating environment for developing, hosting, and managing cloud-based services, establishes a foundation that allows customers to easily move their applications from on-premises locations to the cloud. With Windows Azure, customers benefit from increased agility, a very scalable platform, and reduced costs. Microsoft's cloud strategy has three broad tenets:

- Flexibility of choice, based on business needs, for deploying services
- Enterprise-class services with no compromises on availability, reliability, or security
- Consistent, connected experiences across devices and platforms

Windows Azure is a key component of Microsoft's cloud strategy.

Windows Azure builds on Microsoft's many years of experience running online services for millions of users and on our long history of building platforms for developers. We focused on making the transition from on-premises to the cloud easy for both programmers and IT professionals. Their existing skills and experience are exactly what they need to start using the Windows Azure platform.

Microsoft is committed to Windows Azure, and will continue to expand it as we learn how all our customers around the globe, from the largest enterprises to the smallest ISVs, use it. One of the advantages of an online platform is that it allows us to introduce innovations quickly.

I'm excited to introduce this first guide from the Microsoft patterns & practices team, proof of our commitment to help customers be successful with the Windows Azure platform. Whether you're new to Windows Azure, or if you're already using it, you'll find the Windows Azure architecture guide a great source of things to consider. I encourage you to get started exploring Microsoft's public cloud and to stay tuned for further guidance from the patterns & practices team.

Sincerely,
Yousef Khalidi
Distinguished Engineer, Windows Azure

Preface

How can a company's applications be scalable and have high availability? To achieve this, along with developing the applications, you must also have an infrastructure that can support them. For example, you may need to add servers or increase the capacities of existing ones, have redundant hardware, add logic to the application to handle distributed computing, and add logic for failovers. You have to do this even if an application is in high demand for only short periods of time. Life becomes even more complicated (and expensive) when you start to consider issues such as network latency and security boundaries.

The cloud offers a solution to this dilemma. The cloud is made up of interconnected servers located in various data centers. However, you see what appears to be a centralized location that someone else hosts and manages. By shifting the responsibility of maintaining an infrastructure to someone else, you're free to concentrate on what matters most: the application. If the cloud has data centers in different geographical areas, you can move your content closer to the people who are using it most. If an application is heavily used in Asia, have an instance running in a data center located there. This kind of flexibility may not be available to you if you have to own all the hardware. Another advantage to the cloud is that it's a "pay as you go" proposition. If you don't need it, you don't have to pay for it. When demand is high, you can scale up, and when demand is low, you can scale back.

Yes, by moving applications to the cloud, you're giving up some control and autonomy, but you're also going to benefit from reduced costs, increased flexibility, and scalable computation and storage. The Windows Azure architecture guide shows you how to do this.

Who This Book Is For

This book is the first volume in a planned series about Windows® Azure™. It demonstrates how you can adapt an existing, on-premises ASP.NET application to one that operates in the cloud. The book is intended for any architect, developer, or information technology (IT) professional who designs, builds, or operates applications and services that are appropriate for the cloud. Although applications do not need to be based on the Microsoft® Windows® operating system to work in Windows Azure, this book is written for people who work with Windows-based systems. You should be familiar with the Microsoft . NET Framework, Microsoft Visual Studio®, ASP.NET, and Microsoft Visual C#®.

Why This Book Is Pertinent Now

In general, the cloud has become a viable option for making your applications accessible to a broad set of customers. In particular, Windows Azure now has in place a complete set of tools for developers and IT professionals. Developers can use the tools they already know, such as Visual Studio, to write their applications. In addition, Windows Azure provides a complete, simulated environment known as the *development fabric*. Developers can use this to write, test, and debug their applications locally before they deploy them to the cloud. There are also tools and an API to manage your Windows Azure accounts. This book shows you how to use all these tools in the context of a common scenario—how to adapt an existing ASP.NET application and deploy it to Windows Azure.

How This Book Is Structured

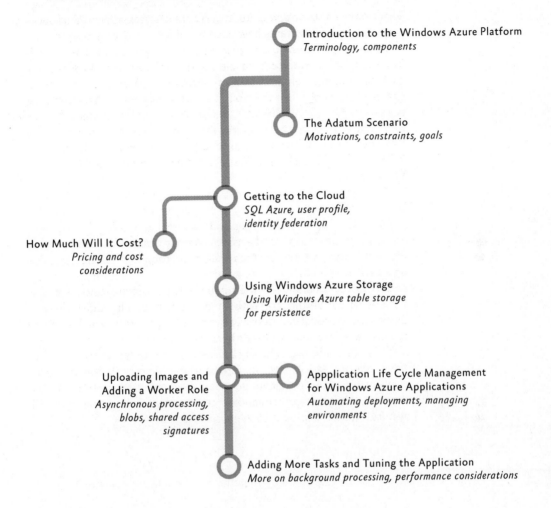

Introduction to the Windows Azure Platform
Terminology, components

The Adatum Scenario
Motivations, constraints, goals

Getting to the Cloud
*SQL Azure, user profile,
identity federation*

How Much Will It Cost?
*Pricing and cost
considerations*

Using Windows Azure Storage
*Using Windows Azure table storage
for persistence*

**Uploading Images and
Adding a Worker Role**
*Asynchronous processing,
blobs, shared access
signatures*

**Appplication Life Cycle Management
for Windows Azure Applications**
*Automating deployments, managing
environments*

Adding More Tasks and Tuning the Application
More on background processing, performance considerations

"Introduction to the Windows Azure Platform" provides an overview of the platform to get you started with Windows Azure. It describes web roles and worker roles, and the different ways you can store data in Windows Azure. It's probably a good idea that you read this before you go to the scenarios.

"The Adatum Scenario" introduces you to the Adatum company and the aExpense application. The following chapters describe how Adatum migrates the aExpense application to the cloud. Reading this chapter will help you understand why Adatum wants to migrate some of its business applications to the cloud, and it describes some of its concerns.

"Phase 1: Getting to the Cloud" describes the first steps that Adatum takes in migrating the aExpense application. Adatum's goal here is simply to get the application working in the cloud, but this includes "big" issues, such as security and storage.

"How Much Will It Cost?" introduces a basic cost model for the aExpense application running on Windows Azure and calculates the estimated annual running costs for the application. This chapter is optional. You don't need to read it before you go on to the following scenarios.

"Phase 2: Automating Deployment and Using Windows Azure Storage" describes how Adatum uses PowerShell scripts and the Microsoft Build Engine (MSBuild) to automate deploying aExpense to Windows Azure. It also describes how Adatum switches from using SQL Azure to Windows Azure Table Storage in the aExpense application and discusses the differences between the two storage models.

"Phase 3: Uploading Images and Adding a Worker Role" describes adding a worker role to the aExpense application and shows how aExpense uses Windows Azure Blob Storage for storing scanned images.

"Application Life Cycle Management for Windows Azure Applications" discusses how to manage developing, testing, and deploying Windows Azure applications. This chapter is optional. You don't need to read it before you go on to the last scenario.

"Phase 4: Adding More Tasks and Tuning the Application" shows how Adatum adds more tasks to the worker role in the aExpense application. In this phase, Adatum also evaluates the results of performance testing the application and makes some changes based on the results.

What You Need to Use the Code

These are the system requirements for running the scenarios:
- Microsoft Windows Vista SP1, Windows 7, or Microsoft Windows Server 2008 (32-bit or 64-bit)
- Microsoft Internet Information Services (IIS) 7.0
- Microsoft .NET Framework 3.5 SP1 or later
- Microsoft Visual Studio® 2008 SP1
- Windows Azure Tools for Microsoft Visual Studio
- Windows Identity Foundation

Who's Who

As mentioned earlier, this book uses a set of scenarios that demonstrates how to move applications to the cloud. A panel of experts comments on the development efforts. The panel includes a cloud specialist, a software architect, a software developer, and an IT professional. The scenarios can be considered from each of these points of view. The following table lists the experts for these scenarios.

Bharath is a cloud specialist. He checks that a cloud-based solution will work for a company and provide tangible benefits. He is a cautious person, for good reasons.

> Moving a single application to the cloud is easy. Realizing the benefits that a cloud-based solution can offer is not always so straight-forward.

Jana is a software architect. She plans the overall structure of an application. Her perspective is both practical and strategic. In other words, she considers not only what technical approaches are needed today, but also what direction a company needs to consider for the future.

> It's not easy to balance the needs of the company, the users, the IT organization, the developers, and the technical platforms we rely on.

Markus is a senior software developer. He is analytical, detail-oriented, and methodical. He's focused on the task at hand, which is building a great cloud-based application. He knows that he's the person who's ultimately responsible for the code.

> I don't care what platform you want to use for the application, I'll make it work.

Poe is an IT professional who's an expert in deploying and running in a corporate data center. Poe has a keen interest in practical solutions; after all, he's the one who gets paged at 3:00 AM when there's a problem.

> Migrating to the cloud involves a big change in the way we manage our applications. I want to make sure our cloud apps are as reliable and secure as our on-premise apps.

If you have a particular area of interest, look for notes provided by the specialists whose interests align with yours.

Acknowledgments

On March 4th, I saw an email from our CEO, Steve Ballmer, in my inbox. I don't normally receive much email from him, so I gave it my full attention. The subject line of the email was: "We are all in," and it summarized the commitment of Microsoft® to cloud computing. If I needed another confirmation of what I already knew, that Microsoft is serious about the cloud, there it was.

My first contact with what eventually became Windows® Azure™, and other components of what is now called the Windows Azure platform, was about three years ago. I was in the Developer & Platform Evangelism (DPE) team, and my job was to explore the world of software delivered as a service. Some of you might even remember a very early mockup I developed in late 2007, called Northwind Hosting. It demonstrated many of the capabilities that the Windows Azure platform offers today. (Watching an initiative I've been involved with since the early days become a reality makes me very, very happy.)

In February 2009, I left DPE and joined the patterns & practices team. My mission was to lead the "cloud program:" a collection of projects that examined the design challenges of building applications for the cloud. When the Windows Azure platform was announced, demand for guidance about it skyrocketed.

As we examined different application development scenarios, it became quite clear that identity management is something you must get right before you can consider anything else. It's especially important if you are a company with a large portfolio of on-premises investments, and you want to move some of those assets to the cloud. This describes many of our customers.

In December 2009, we released *A Guide to Claims-Based Identity and Access Control*. This was patterns & practices's first deliverable, and an important milestone, in our cloud program.

The Windows Azure platform is special in many ways. One is the rate of innovation. The various teams that deliver all of the platform's systems proved that they could rapidly ship new functionality. To keep up with them, I felt we had to develop content very quickly. We decided to run our projects in two-months sprints, each one focused on a specific set of considerations.

This guide is the result of our first sprint and mainly covers a migration scenario: how to move an existing application to the Windows Azure platform. As in the claims guide, we've developed a fictitious case study that explains, step by step, the challenges our customers are likely to encounter.

I want to start by thanking the following subject matter experts and contributors to this guide: Dominic Betts, Scott Densmore, Ryan Dunn, Steve Marx, and Matias Woloski. Dominic has the unusual skill of knowing a subject in great detail and of finding a way to explain it to the rest of us that is precise, complete, and yet simple to understand. Scott brought us a wealth of knowledge about how to build scalable Windows Azure applications, which is what he did before he joined my team. He also brings years of experience about how to build frameworks and tools for developers. I've had the privilege of working with Ryan in previous projects, and I've always benefited from his acuity, insights, and experience. As a Windows Azure evangelist, he's been able to show us what customers with very real requirements need. Steve is a technical strategist for Windows Azure. He's been instrumental in shaping this guide. We rely on him to show us not just what the platform can do today but how it will evolve. This is important because we want to provide guidance today that is aligned with longer-term goals. Last but not least, Matias is a veteran of many projects with me. He's been involved with Windows Azure since the very first day, and his efforts have been invaluable in creating this guide.

As it happens with all our written content, we have sample code for most of the chapters. They demonstrate what we talk about in the guide. Many thanks to the project's development and test teams for providing a good balance of technically sound, focused and simple-to-understand code: Federico Boerr (Southworks), Scott Densmore, Masashi Narumoto, Kirthi Royadu (Infosys Ltd.), Lavanya Selvaraj (Infosys Ltd.), and Matias Woloski (Southworks).

Our guides must not only be technically accurate but also entertaining and interesting to read. This is no simple task, and I want to thank Dominic Betts, RoAnn Corbisier, Colin Campbell, Roberta Leibovitz, and Tina Burden from the writing and editing team for excelling at this.

The visual design concept used for this guide was originally developed by Roberta Leibovitz and Colin Campbell (Modeled Computation LLC) for *A Guide to Claims-Based Identity and Access Control*. Based on the excellent responses we received, we decided to reuse it for this book. The book design was created by John Hubbard (Eson). The cartoon faces were drawn by the award-winning Seattle-based cartoonist Ellen Forney. The technical illustrations were adapted from my Tablet PC mockups by Rob Nance.

All of our guides are reviewed, commented upon, scrutinized, and criticized by a large number of customers, partners, and colleagues. We also received feedback from the larger community through our CodePlex website. The Windows Azure platform is broad and spans many disciplines. We were very fortunate to have the intellectual power of a very diverse and skillful group of readers available to us.

I also want to thank all of these people who volunteered their time and expertise on our early content and drafts. Among them, I want to mention the exceptional contributions of David Aiken, Graham Astor (Avanade), Edward Bakker (Inter Access), Vivek Bhatnagar, Patrick Butler Monterde (Microsoft), Shy Cohen, James Conard, Brian Davis (Longscale), Aashish Dhamdhere (Windows Azure, Microsoft), Andreas Erben (DAENET), Giles Frith , Eric L. Golpe (Microsoft), Johnny Halife (Southworks), Alex Homer, Simon Ince, Joshy Joseph, Andrew Kimball, Milinda Kotelawele (Longscale), Mark Kottke (Microsoft), Chris Lowndes (Avanade), Dianne O'Brien (Windows Azure, Microsoft), Steffen Vorein (Avanade), Michael Wood (Strategic Data Systems).

I hope you find this guide useful!

Eugenio Pace
Senior Program Manager – *patterns & practices*
Microsoft Corporation
Redmond, May 2010

1 Introduction
TO THE
WINDOWS AZURE PLATFORM

The Microsoft® Windows® Azure™ technology platform provides on-demand, cloud-based computing, where the *cloud* is a set of interconnected computing resources located in one or more data centers. Currently, the Windows Azure platform is available in data centers in the United States, Europe, and Asia. Developers can use the cloud to deploy and run applications and to store data. On-premises applications can still use cloud–based resources. For example, an application located on an on-premises server, a rich client that runs on a desktop computer, or one that runs on a mobile device can use storage that is located on the cloud.

The Windows Azure platform abstracts hardware resources through virtualization. Each application that is deployed to Windows Azure runs on one or more Virtual Machines (VMs). These deployed applications behave as though they were on a dedicated computer, although they might share physical resources such as disk space, network I/O, or CPU cores with other VMs on the same physical host. A key benefit of an abstraction layer above the physical hardware is portability and scalability. Virtualizing a service allows it to be moved to any number of physical hosts in the data center. By combining virtualization technologies, commodity hardware, multi-tenancy, and aggregation of demand, Microsoft can achieve economies of scale. These generate higher data center utilization (that is, more useful work-per-dollar hardware cost) and, subsequently, savings that are passed along to you.

Virtualization also allows you to have both vertical scalability and horizontal scalability. Vertical scalability means that, as demand increases, you can increase the number of resources, such as CPU cores or memory, on a specific VM. Horizontal scalability means that you can add more instances of VMs that are copies of existing services. All these instances are load balanced at the network level so that incoming requests are distributed among them.

At the time of this writing, the Windows Azure platform includes three main components: Windows Azure, the Windows Azure platform AppFabric, and SQL Azure.

Windows Azure provides the following capabilities:

- A Microsoft Windows® Server-based computing environment for applications
- Persistent storage for both structured and unstructured data, as well as asynchronous messaging

The Windows Azure platform AppFabric provides two services:

- Service Bus, which helps you to connect applications that are on-premises or in the public cloud, regardless of the network topology
- Access Control Service, which manages authorization and authentication for Representational State Transfer (REST)–based Web services with security tokens

SQL Azure is essentially SQL Server® provided as a service in the cloud.

The platform also includes various management services that allow you to control all these resources, either through a web-based user interface (a web portal) or programmatically. In most cases, there's REST-based API that can be used to define how your services will work. Most management tasks that can be performed through the web portal can also be done through the API. Finally, there's a comprehensive set of tools and software development kits (SDKs) that allow you to develop, test, and deploy your applications. For example, you can develop and test your applications in a simulated local environment, named the *development fabric*. Most tools are also integrated into development environments such as Microsoft Visual Studio®. In addition, there are also third-party management tools available.

The Windows Azure Platform

In Windows Azure, the compute environment processes requests, and the storage environment holds data reliably. An internal subsystem, known as the *Windows Azure Fabric Controller (FC)* manages all compute and storage resources, deploys new services, and monitors the health of each deployed service. When a service fails, the FC provisions the necessary resources and re-deploys the service. Another component of the Windows Azure platform is SQL Azure. SQL Azure is a relational database in the cloud. Essentially, SQL Azure is a large subset of SQL Server hosted by Microsoft and offered as a service. Although SQL Azure is complementary to Windows Azure storage services, they are not the same.

At the time of this writing, the Windows Azure platform App Fabric provides two services: the service bus and the access control services.

The service bus allows you to connect applications and services, no matter where they are located. For example, you can connect an on-premises application that is behind the corporate firewall to a service that runs in the cloud. It implements common message and communications patterns, such as events, one-way messages, publish and subscribe, remote procedure call (RPC)–style message exchanges, and tunnels for streamed data. The access control service allows you to manage identity in the cloud for REST-based services. It implements a token-issuing service that also provides token transformation capabilities. The Windows Azure platform AppFabric isn't discussed in this guidance. For more information, see the references at the end of this chapter. Remember that the Windows Azure platform AppFabric is not the same as the Windows Azure Fabric Controller.

In addition to these components, the Windows Azure platform also provides diagnostics services for activities such as monitoring an application's health.

The Windows Azure Fabric Controller and the Windows Azure platform AppFabric are not the same! The Fabric Controller is an internal system used by Windows Azure to provision, monitor, and manage services that run in Windows Azure.

All storage and management subsystems in Windows Azure use REST-based interfaces. They are not dependent on any .NET Framework or Microsoft Windows® operating system technology. Any technology that can issue HTTP or HTTPS requests can access Windows Azure's facilities.

Typically, applications that run in Windows Azure have multiple instances. Each of these instances runs in a Windows Virtual Machine (VM) that is created and managed by Windows Azure. Currently, you cannot access these VMs the way you can if create a VM with an application such as Virtual Server or Virtual PC. Windows Azure controls them for you.

To get started with Windows Azure platform, go to http://www.windowsazure.com.

Windows Azure Compute

An application that runs on Windows Azure is referred to as a *hosted service*. Typically, a hosted service contains different computational resources that collectively process information and interact with each other and the external world. Hosted services in Windows Azure are said to contain roles, and there are currently two roles available: *a worker role* and *a web role*.

Worker roles are general-purpose code hosts. They are frequently used for long-running tasks that are non-interactive, but you can host any type of workload in them. Worker roles are general enough to host even complete application platforms such as Microsoft Internet Information Services (IIS) or Apache Tomcat. Windows Azure initiates worker roles and, like Windows services, they run all the time.

You can think of web roles as special cases of worker roles that have IIS 7 enabled by default. Therefore, they can host web applications and web services. Figure 1 illustrates web and worker roles.

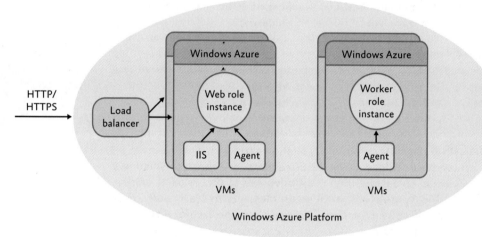

FIGURE 1
Web roles and worker roles

Typically, a web role instance accepts incoming HTTP or HTTPS requests over ports 80 and 443. These public ports are referred to as public endpoints. All public endpoints are automatically load balanced at the network level. Both worker roles and web roles can make outbound TCP connections and can also open endpoints for incoming connections. In addition to the load-balanced public endpoints, instances can open internal endpoints. These internal endpoints are neither load-balanced, nor publically visible to the Internet. Instead, internal endpoints can be used for synchronous communication among instances and roles.

The VMs that run both web role and worker role instances also run a Windows Azure agent. This agent exposes an API that lets an instance interact with the Windows Azure FC. For example, an instance can use the agent to enumerate the public and internal endpoints in the VM instance it's running in or to discover run-time configuration settings.

An application deployed in a web role can be implemented with ASP.NET, Windows Communication Foundation (WCF), or any technology that works with IIS. For example, you can host a Hypertext Preprocessor (PHP) application on Windows Azure because IIS supports it through *Fast CGI*, which is a protocol that interfaces interactive applications with a web server. Most web role applications are optimized for workloads that follow a request-reply pattern, where the time between a request and a response is ideally very short.

A key consideration for the scalability of web roles is session management. In standard ASP.NET applications, there is some way to store session state. For example, an online store may keep track of a shopping cart. Similar to web farms, storing session state in memory on each server instance is a problem for web role–based websites because there's no guarantee that users will be directed to the same web role instance each time they make a request. Instead, you maintain state information in someplace other than the web role instance such as Windows Azure storage, SQL Azure, in a cookie that you pass back to the client, or in hidden form elements.

One of the most common application patterns in Windows Azure is for a web role to receive incoming requests and then use Windows Azure queues to pass them to the worker role to process. The worker role periodically looks in the queue for messages to see if there is any work to do. If there is, it performs the task. The web role typically retrieves completed work from persistent storage, such as a blob or a table. Figure 2 illustrates this typical design pattern.

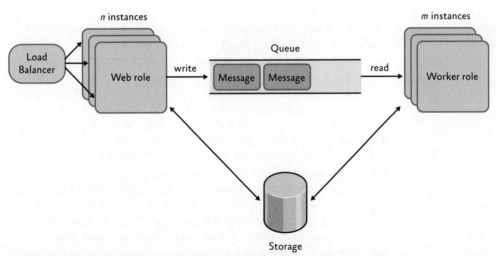

FIGURE 2
Typical application pattern for web roles and worker roles

This is a simple and common interaction between a web role and a worker role, but there are many other possibilities. For example, you can use WCF to link web roles and worker roles.

Another function of the agent that runs on the web and worker roles is to maintain a heartbeat with the FC. The FC monitors the health of the VMs and the physical servers. If an application becomes unresponsive because of an error in its code, or if the underlying hardware of an instance fails, the FC takes whatever action is appropriate to recover. In the case of an application that crashes, the FC might simply restart the instance. In the more extreme case of a hardware error on the underlying physical host, the FC attempts to move the affected instances to another physical machine in the data center. At all times, the FC attempts to keep as many instances running as you specified when you configured the application. There currently are no auto-scaling capabilities. You are responsible for specifying the number of instances of any compute resource on Windows Azure, either through the web portal or with the management API.

Windows Azure Storage

Windows Azure provides scalable storage services that store both structured and unstructured data. The storage services are considered to be scalable for two reasons:

- An application can scale to store many hundreds of terabytes of data.
- The storage services can scale out your data access for better performance, depending on the usage pattern.

Storage services are independent of any hosted services, though they are often used in conjunction with them. Access to Windows Azure storage is with a REST-based API. This means that many clients that support the HTTP stack can access storage services. In practice, co-locating your data with services that run in Windows Azure achieves the best performance. Like hosted services, the storage services are also fault-tolerant and highly available. Each bit of data stored in Windows Azure storage is replicated both within the data center and the geographic region. Data is continuously scanned for bit decay and replicas of your data are maintained (currently, there are three copies).

All data is accessed with HTTP requests that follow REST conventions. The .NET Framework includes many libraries that interact with REST-based services at different abstraction levels, such as WCF Data Services, and direct HTTP calls through the **WebRequest** class. The Windows Azure SDK also contains specialized client libraries that provide domain models for all of the Windows Azure services. REST-based services are also used with many other platforms, such as JAVA, PHP, and Ruby. Almost every programming stack that can handle HTTP requests can interact with Windows Azure storage. There are four types of Windows Azure storage: blobs, drives, tables, and queues. To access Windows Azure storage, you must have a storage account that you create with the Windows Azure portal web interface at http://windows.azure.com.

A storage account is associated with a specific geographical location. Currently, each storage account can hold up to 100 terabytes of data, which can be made up of a combination of blobs, tables, queues, and drives. You can have as many storage accounts as you like, though, by default, you can create up to five accounts.

By default, all access to Windows Azure storage must be authenticated. Each storage account has two 256-bit symmetric keys.

BLOBS

Generally, blobs provide storage for large pieces of data, such as images, video, documents, and code. Each storage account in a subscription can have any number of *containers*, where each container can hold any number of blobs. Storage is limited at the account level, not by any specific container or blob. Blobs are referenced with URLs that are created in the following format:

http(s)://<storage account name>.blob.core.windows.net/<container>/<blob name>

Windows Azure blob storage supports the notion of a *root container*. This is useful when you need to access blobs by specifying just the domain name. The reserved name *$root* denotes this special case. The following URL identifies a blob named "mypicture.jpg" that appears under an account named "myaccount":

http://myaccount.blob.core.windows.net/$root/mypicture.jpg

This is equivalent to the following:

http://myaccount.blob.core.windows.net/mypicture.jpg

You can name blobs so that they appear to belong to a hierarchical namespace, but in reality, the namespace is flat. For example, the following is a blob reference that seems to imply a hierarchical structure:

http://myaccount.blob.core.windows.net/pictures/trips/seattle/spaceneedle.jpg

You could mistakenly assume a hierarchy or folder structure with folders named "pictures", "trips", and "seattle", but actually, all the path segments are the name of the blob itself. In other words, the con-

Silverlight access policy files are a perfect example of where root containers are useful.

tainer's name is "pictures" and the blob's name is "trips/seattle/spac-eneedle.jpg".

Both containers and the blobs themselves can optionally store metadata in the form of a collection of name/value pairs, up to a maximum size of 8 kilobytes (KB). In addition to the **Create**, **Update**, and **Delete** operations, you can also perform more specialized operations on blobs such as **Copy**, **Snapshot**, or **Lease.**

Containers act as a security boundary in blob storage. By default, all access to blob storage requires knowledge of a secret key. However, you can set an access policy on the container to change this behavior to allow anonymous access. Valid access policies are the container-level access policy and the blob-only access policy. Container-level access allows you to enumerate and discover all blobs within the container. Blob-only access requires explicit knowledge of the blob Uniform Resource Identifier (URI). If the access policy is removed, the default behavior that requires knowledge of the key resumes.

Windows Azure provides a content delivery network (CDN) for efficient distribution of blob content. The CDN stores frequently accessed blobs closer to the application that uses it. For example, if a video is particularly popular with users in Asia, the CDN moves the blob to a server that is geographically close to these users. The CDN is an optional feature of blobs that you must explicitly enable. Using this feature may affect your billing.

Figure 3 illustrates how blobs are stored. An account holds blob containers. There can be more than one container associated with an account. The containers hold the blobs.

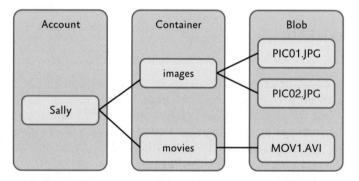

FIGURE 3
Blob storage

Blobs can be divided into two types: block blobs and page blobs.

Block Blobs

Each block blob can store up to 200 gigabytes (GB), which is divided into data blocks of up to 4 megabytes (MB) each. Block blobs are optimized for streaming workloads. They work well for large pieces of data such as streaming video, images, documents, and code. Block blob operations are optimized to safely upload large amounts of information. For example, you can use the API to upload blocks of data in parallel. Also, if there is a failure, you can resume uploads of specific blocks instead of the entire dataset.

For example, if you uploaded a 10 GB file to blob storage, you could split it into blocks of up to 4 MB in size. You would then use the **PutBlock** operation to upload each block independently (or possibly in parallel with other blocks for increased throughput). Finally, you would write all these blocks into a readable blob with the **PutBlock-List** operation. Figure 4 illustrates this example.

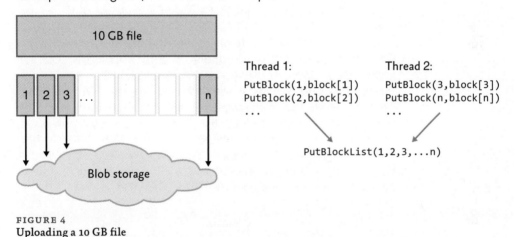

FIGURE 4
Uploading a 10 GB file

Page Blobs

Page blobs have some predefined maximum size, up to 1 terabyte, and consist of an array of *pages*, where each page is 512 bytes. Page blobs are optimized for random access read/write I/O. Write operations, such as the **PutPage** method must be aligned to a page. This means that data is written to offsets that are multiples of 512 bytes. In contrast, read operations, such as the **GetPage** method, can occur on any address that is within a valid range. You are charged for page blobs by the amount of information that they actually contain, not by the amount of reserved space. If you provision a 1 GB page blob that contains 2 pages, you are only charged for 1 KB of data. Figure 5 illustrates basic page blob read and write operations.

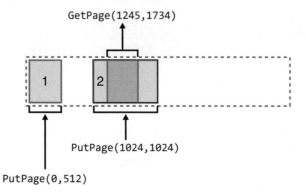

FIGURE 5
Basic read and write operations

WINDOWS AZURE DRIVES
Windows Azure drives are page blobs that are formatted as NTFS single-volume virtual hard drives. A single role instance can mount a drive in exclusive read/write mode or many instances can mount a single drive in read-only mode. There is no way to combine the two options. Typically, one instance mounts the drive in read/write mode and periodically takes a snapshot of the drive. This snapshot can then be simultaneously mounted in read-only mode by other instances.

Because the underlying storage for a Windows Azure drive is a page blob, after the drive is mounted by a compute node, all information written by this node is persisted in the blob. Writing to a blob is possible after acquiring a *lease* on the drive. A lease is one of Windows Azure storage's concurrency control mechanisms. It is, in essence, a lock on a blob. Windows Azure drives are useful for legacy applications that rely on the NTFS file system and on standard I/O libraries. All operations on page blobs are also available for Windows Azure drives.

Figure 6 illustrates a Windows Azure drive.

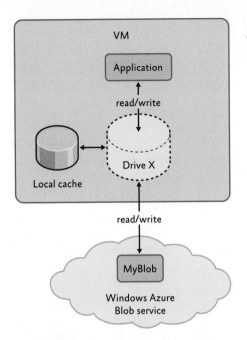

FIGURE 6
Windows Azure drive

A Windows Azure drive is accessible to code that runs in a role. The data written to a Windows Azure drive is stored in a page blob that is defined within the Windows Azure Blob service and cached on the local file system.

WINDOWS AZURE TABLES

Windows Azure tables provide scalable structured storage. Tables are associated with a storage account. Windows Azure tables are not like the tables in a typical relational database. They don't implement relationships and don't have a schema. Instead, each entity stored in a table can have a different set of properties made up of different types, such as **string** or **int**. Tables use *optimistic concurrency*, based on time stamps, for updates and deletions. Optimistic concurrency assumes that concurrency violations occur infrequently and simply disallows any updates or deletions that cause a concurrency violation. Figure 7 illustrates table storage.

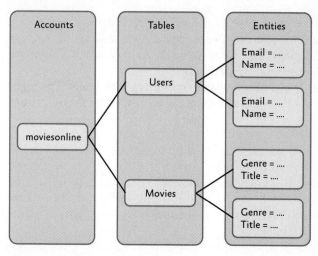

FIGURE 7
Windows Azure table storage

There are three properties that all entities in a table have: a **Partition-Key, a RowKey** and the system-controlled property, **LastUpdate. Entities** are identified by the **PartitionKey** and the **RowKey** properties. **The LastUpdate** property is used for optimistic concurrency.

Windows Azure monitors the **PartitionKey** property and automatically scales tables if there is sufficient activity. It can potentially scale tables up to thousands of storage nodes by distributing the entities in the table. The **PartitionKey** also ensures that some set of related entities always stay together. This means that it is important to choose a good value for the key. The combination of the **PartitionKey** and the **RowKey** uniquely identifies any given entity instance in the table.

A query against a Windows Azure table that specifies both the **PartitionKey** and **RowKey** properties returns a single entity. Any other type of query could potentially return many entities because uniqueness is not guaranteed. Windows Azure table storage returns data in pages (currently, up to 1,000 entities are returned for each query). If there's more data to retrieve, the returned result set includes a continuation token that can be used to get the next page of data. Continuation tokens are returned until there's no more data available.

Tables don't currently support any aggregation functions, such as **Sum** or **Count**. Even though you can count rows or sum columns, most of these operations are resolved on the client side and involve scanning the entire table contents, which could be very expensive. You should consider other approaches, such as pre-computing and storing the values that you need, or providing approximations.

Transactions are supported within a single partition in a single table. For example, you can create, delete, and update entities in a single atomic operation. This is referred to as a batch operation. Batches are limited to 4 MB payloads.

There are various APIs available to interact with tables. The highest level ones use WCF Data Services. At the lowest level, you can use the REST endpoints that are exposed by Windows Azure.

WINDOWS AZURE QUEUES

Unlike blobs and tables, which are used to store data, queues serve another purpose. A primary use is to allow web roles to communicate with worker roles, typically for notifications and to schedule work. Queues provide persistent asynchronous messaging, where each message is up to 8 KB long.

Windows Azure queues are **not related to Microsoft Message Queuing (MSMQ)**.

Applications that retrieve messages from queues should be designed to be *idempotent,* because the messages can be processed more than once. Idempotency means that an operation can be performed multiple times without changing the result. Applications that retrieve messages should also be designed to handle poison messages. A *poison message* contains malformed data that causes the queue processor to throw an exception. The result is that the message isn't processed, stays in the queue, and the next attempt to process it once again fails.

Figure 8 illustrates queue storage. Accounts can contain queues that, in turn, contain messages.

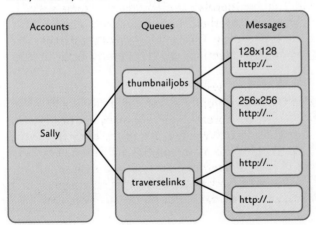

FIGURE 8
Queue storage

The SDK includes a domain model that implements a higher-level abstraction of a queue. You can also interact with queues through a REST endpoint.

SQL Azure

SQL Azure is a cloud-based relational database management system (RDBMS). It currently focuses on the features required to perform transactions. For example, it provides indexes, views, triggers, and stored procedures. Applications that access SQL Server locally should be able to use SQL Azure with few, if any, changes. Customers can also use on-premises software, such as SQL Server Reporting Services, to work with SQL Azure.

You can connect to SQL Azure in a variety of ways, such as ADO. NET, PHP, and Open Database Connectivity (ODBC). This means that the way that you develop database applications today are the same as for SQL Azure. Essentially, if you have a database that you relocate to the cloud, you simply change the connection string.

Applications can either be located in the cloud, along with the database, or they can be located on-premises, and connect to a database that is in the cloud. The first option is known as *code near* and the second is known as *code far.*

No matter where the application is located, it accesses data with a protocol named Tabular Data Stream (TDS) over TCP/IP. This is the same protocol that is used to access a local SQL Server database.

SQL Azure includes a security feature that restricts access to the database to particular IP address ranges. You specify the IP addresses of the expected incoming connections and reject all others at the network level.

To access SQL Azure, you must create an account at http://sql. azure.com. Each account can have one or more logical servers, which are implemented as multiple physical servers within a geographical location. Each logical server can contain one or more logical databases, which are implemented as replicated, partitioned data across multiple physical servers.

You first create a database with the SQL Azure server administration interface, which is available on the web portal. You can also use tools such as SQL Server Management Studio to create databases, add elements such as user-defined objects, tables, views, and indexes, or to change the firewall settings.

SQL Azure is available in three database sizes: 1 GB, 10 GB, and 50 GB. Your bill is based on the size of the database, not on the amount of information you actually store.

Management Services

A main goal of Windows Azure is to make life simpler for application owners. One of the ways it does this is by providing a layer of automated service management. With this service, developers create the application and deploy it to the cloud. Developers also configure the service settings and constraints. After these tasks are performed, Windows Azure runs the service and maintains its health.

Windows Azure also provides capabilities to perform a number of operations, such as monitoring your applications and managing your storage accounts, hosted services, service deployments, and affinity groups. You can either use a web portal for these operations or perform them programmatically with a REST-based API. The API uses a different authentication mechanism than the web portal. All programmatic calls use X509 client certificates for authentication. Users can upload any valid X509 certificate to the Windows Azure developer portal and then use it as a client certificate when making API requests.

> **Note**: *The Windows Azure management API described here is specifically for Windows Azure components such as compute and storage. Other services in the platform (such as SQL Azure and the AppFabric) have their own set of management interfaces.*

Windows Azure Subscription and Billing Model

Figure 9 illustrates the current Windows Azure billing configuration for a standard subscription.

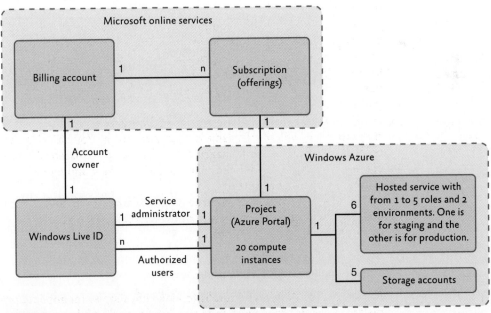

FIGURE 9
Windows Azure billing configuration for a standard subscription

To use Windows Azure, you first create a billing account by signing up for Microsoft Online Services, which manages subscriptions to all Microsoft services. Windows Azure is one of these, but there are others, such as Microsoft SharePoint® and hosted Exchange. You create a billing account on the Microsoft Online Services customer portal. Every billing account has a single account owner who is identified with a Windows Live® ID. The account owner can create and manage subscriptions, view billing information and usage data, and specify the service administrator for each subscription. The service administrator manages services and also deployments. There is one service administrator for each project. The account owner and the service administrator can be (and in many cases should be) different Live IDs.

After you have the billing account, you can select Windows Azure from the subscription offerings. When you buy a subscription, you enter a subscription name. This is the name of the Azure project. After buying the subscription, you can activate the Windows Azure service and specify the service administrator. For each billing account, you can have as many subscriptions as you want.

Next, go to the Windows Azure Portal at http://windows.azure. com and sign in. You will see the Windows Azure Portal home page with a project that has the name you gave when you created the subscription. On the home page, you can create services for your project. A service is either a hosted service or a storage account.

By default, each project is limited to twenty compute instances. Each project can have up to six hosted services. Hosted services are spaces where applications are deployed. Each hosted service has from one to five roles. These can be any combination of web roles and worker roles. In Visual Studio, you can configure a role for the number of instances and the size of the VM. VMs can be designated as small, medium, large, and extra large. The definitions of what these mean are located at http://msdn.microsoft.com/en-us/library/ee814754.aspx. Briefly, a small VM corresponds to 1 CPU core, a medium VM corresponds to 2 CPU cores, a large VM corresponds to 4 CPU cores, and an extra large VM corresponds to 8 CPU cores. A *core* is the processing portion of a CPU, exclusive of the cache. A hosted service is always associated with an URL.

A hosted service also has a staging environment and a production environment. Finally, a project can have up to five storage accounts. These are also shared among all the hosted services in the subscription. If you need more computing power or storage capacity, you can arrange this through Microsoft Online Services.

The number of CPU cores for a hosted service is number of roles X instance count X number of CPU cores for the selected VM size. For example, if you have one hosted service with two roles, where each role has one instance and is a small VM, the number of CPU cores is 1 x 2 x 1 = 2. As another example, if you have five hosted services, each with one role, two instances of that role and a medium VM, the number of CPU cores is 5 x 1 x 2 x 2 = 20. This is the default limit for CPU cores per project.

For storage, you can have up to five accounts, each of which can contain up to 100 terabytes of data. This can be any combination of blobs, tables, and queues.

Another point to remember is that you are billed for role resources that are used by a deployed service, even if the roles on those services are not running. If you don't want to get charged for a service, delete the deployments associated with the service.

ESTIMATING YOUR COSTS

Windows Azure charges for how you consume services such as compute time, storage, and bandwidth. Compute time charges are calculated by an hourly rate as well as a rate for the instance size. Storage charges are based on the number of gigabytes and the number of transactions. Prices for data transfer vary according to the region you are in and generally apply to transfers between the Microsoft data centers and your premises, but not on transfers within the same data center. There are also various purchasing models, such as the consumption model and the subscription model. For a description of the different pricing models and any special offers, go to http://www.microsoft.com/windowsazure/pricing/.

If you want to estimate your costs for using Windows Azure, you can use the Microsoft Windows Azure platform TCO and ROI Calculator, where TCO is total cost of ownership and ROI is return on investment. The tool is located at http://www.microsoft.com/windowsazure/tco/. Using information you provide about your company and the application, the tool can help you estimate the correct configuration and its costs, the costs of migrating an application to Windows Azure, and compare on-premises and Windows Azure application delivery costs.

More Information

There is a great deal of information about the Windows Azure platform in the form of documentation, training videos, and white papers. Here are some Webs sites you can visit to get started:

- The portal to information about Microsoft Windows Azure is at http://www.microsoft.com/windowsazure/. It has links to white papers, tools such as the Windows Azure SDK, and many other resources. You can also sign up for a Windows Azure account here.
- The Windows Azure platform Training Kit contains hands-on labs to get you quickly started. You can download it at http://www.microsoft.com/downloads/details. aspx?FamilyID=413E88F8-5966-4A83-B309-53B7B77EDF78&displaylang=en.
- Ryan Dunn and Steve Marx have a series of Channel 9 discussions about Azure at Cloud Cover, located at http://channel9.msdn.com/shows/Cloud+Cover/.
- Find answers to your questions on the Windows Azure Forum at http://social.msdn.microsoft.com/Forums/ en-US/windowsazure/threads.
- Steve Marx is a Windows Azure technical strategist. His blog is at http://blog.smarx.com/. It is a great source of news and information on Windows Azure.
- Ryan Dunn is the Windows Azure technical evangelist. His blog is at http://dunnry.com/blog.
- Eugenio Pace, a program manager in the Microsoft patterns & practices group, is creating a series of guides on Windows Azure, to which this documentation belongs. To learn more about the series, see his blog at http://blogs.msdn.com/ eugeniop.
- Scott Densmore, lead developer in the Microsoft patterns & practices group, writes about developing applications for Windows Azure on his blog at http://scottdensmore. typepad.com/.
- Jim Nakashima is a program manager in the group that builds tools for Windows Azure. His blog is full of technical details and tips. It is at http://blogs.msdn.com/jnak/.
- Code and documentation for the patterns & practice guidance project is available on the CodePlex Windows Azure Guidance site at http://wag.codeplex.com/.

2   The Adatum Scenario

This chapter introduces a fictitious company named Adatum. The chapter describes Adatum's current infrastructure, its software portfolio, and why Adatum wants to move some of its applications to the Windows® Azure™ platform. As with any company considering this process, there are many issues to take into account and challenges to be met, particularly because Adatum has not used the cloud before. The chapters that follow this one show, step-by-step, how Adatum modifies its expense tracking and reimbursement system, aExpense, so that it can be deployed to Windows Azure.

The Adatum Company

Adatum is a manufacturing company of 5,000 employees that mostly uses Microsoft® technologies and tools. It also has some legacy systems built on other platforms, such as AS400 and UNIX. As you would expect, Adatum developers are knowledgeable about various Microsoft products, including .NET Framework, ASP.NET, SQL Server® database software, Windows Server® operating system, and Microsoft Visual Studio® development system. Employees in Adatum's IT department are proficient at tasks such as setting up and maintaining Microsoft Active Directory® directory service and using System Center.

Adatum uses many different applications. Some are externally facing, while others are used exclusively by its employees. The importance of these applications ranges from "peripheral" to "critical," with many lying between the two extremes. A significant portion of Adatum's IT budget is allocated to maintaining applications that are either of mid-level or peripheral importance.

Adatum wants to change this allocation. Its aim is to spend more money on the services that differentiate it from its competitors and less on those that don't. Adatum's competitive edge results from assets, such as its efficient supply chain and excellent quality controls, and not from how effectively it handles its internal e-mail. Adatum wants efficient e-mail, but it's looking for more economical ways to provide this so that it can spend most of its budget on the systems that directly affect its customers. Adatum believes that one way to achieve this optimization is to selectively deploy applications to the cloud.

ADATUM'S CHALLENGES

Adatum faces several challenges. Currently, deploying new on-premises applications takes too long, considering how quickly its business changes and how efficient its competitors are. The timeframe for acquiring, provisioning, and deploying even a simple application can be at least several weeks. No matter the application's complexity, requirements must be analyzed, procurement processes must be initiated, requests for proposals may need to be sent to vendors, networks must be configured, and so on. Adatum must be able to respond to its customers' demands more rapidly than the current procedures allow.

Another issue is that much of Adatum's infrastructure is used inefficiently. The majority of its servers are underutilized, and it's difficult to deploy new applications with the requisite service-level agreements (SLA) to the existing hardware. Virtual machines are appropriate in some cases, but they are not appropriate in all cases. This inefficiency means that Adatum's capital is committed to an underutilized infrastructure when it could be better used elsewhere in the business.

A final issue is that less critical applications typically get less attention from the IT staff. It is only when the application fails or cannot keep up with demand that anyone takes notice. By this time, the problem is expensive to fix, both in terms of IT time and in inefficient use of the users' time.

Adatum believes that by deploying some of its applications to a public cloud such as the Windows Azure platform, it can take advantage of economies of scale, promote standardization of its applications, and have automated processes for managing them. Most importantly, Adatum believes that this will make it more effective at addressing its customers' needs, a more effective competitor, and a better investment for its shareholders.

ADATUM'S GOALS AND CONCERNS

One of Adatum's goals is to improve the experience of all users of its applications. At a minimum, applications in the cloud should perform as well as their on-premises counterparts. The hope, though, is that they will perform better. Many of its applications are used more at some times than at others. For example, employees use the salary tool once every two weeks but rarely at other times. They would benefit if the applications had increased responsiveness during peak periods. This sensitivity to demand is known as *dynamic scalability*. However, on-premises applications that are associated with specific servers don't provide this flexibility. Adatum can't afford to run as many servers as are needed during peak times because this hardware is dormant the rest of the time. If these applications were located in the cloud, it would be easy to scale them depending on the demand.

Another goal is to expand the ways that users can access Adatum's applications. Currently, applications are only accessible from the intranet. Publishing them to the Internet is difficult and requires increased security. It also requires a virtual private network (VPN), which users often don't want to use because of the additional complexity that a VPN can introduce. Applications that are located in the public cloud are, by definition, available on the Internet. However, the public cloud also raises questions about security. In addition, many of Adatum's applications use Windows authentication so that users aren't required to enter application-specific credentials. Adatum is concerned that its users would need special credentials for each application in the public cloud.

A third goal is that at least some of Adatum's applications should be *portable*. Portability means that the application can be moved back and forth between a hosted data center to an on-premises data center without any modifications to the application's code or its operations. If both options are available, the risks that Adatum incurs if it does use the cloud are reduced.

In addition to its concerns about security, Adatum has two other issues. First, it would like to avoid a massive retraining program for its IT staff. Second, very few of Adatum's applications are truly isolated from other systems. Most have various dependencies. Adatum has put a great of deal effort into integrating its systems, even if not all of them operate on the same platform. It is unsure how these dependencies affect operations if some systems are moved to the public cloud.

ADATUM'S STRATEGY

Adatum is an innovative company and open to new technologies, but it takes carefully considered steps when it implements them. Adatum's plan is to evaluate the viability of moving to the cloud by starting with some of its simpler applications. It hopes to gain some initial experience, and then expand on what it has learned. This strategy can be described as "try, learn, fail fast, and then optimize." Adatum has decided to start with its aExpense application.

The aExpense Application

The aExpense application allows Adatum's employees to submit, track, and process business expenses. Everyone in Adatum uses this application to request reimbursements. Although aExpense is not a critical application, it is important. Employees can tolerate occasional hours of downtime, but prolonged unavailability isn't acceptable.

Adatum's policy is that employees must submit their expenses before the end of each month. The majority of employees don't submit their expenses until the last two business days. This causes relatively high demands during a short time period. The infrastructure that supports the aExpense application is scaled for average use across the month instead of for this peak demand. As a result, when the majority of employees try to submit their expenses during the last two business days, the system is slow and the employees complain.

The application is deployed in Adatum's data center and is available to users on the intranet. While traveling, employees access it through a VPN. There have been requests for publishing aExpense directly to the Internet, but it's never happened.

The application stores a great deal of information because most expense receipts must be scanned and then stored for seven years. For this reason, the data stores used by aExpense are frequently backed up.

The application is representative of many other applications in Adatum's portfolio so it's a good test case for using the cloud. Moving the aExpense application to the Windows Azure platform will expose many of the challenges Adatum is likely to encounter as it expands the number of applications that it relocates to the cloud.

THE AEXPENSE ARCHITECTURE

Figure 1 illustrates the aExpense architecture.

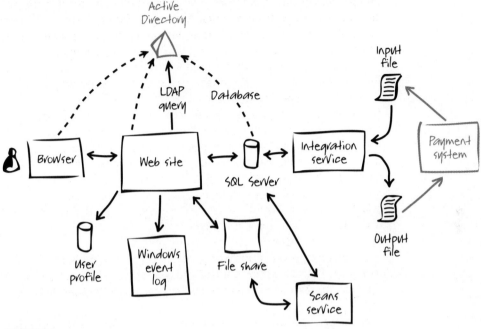

The architecture is straightforward and one that many other applications use. aExpense is an ASP.NET application and employees use a browser to interact with it. The application uses Windows authentication for security. To store user preferences, it relies on ASP.NET membership and profile providers. Exceptions and logs are implemented with Enterprise Library's Exception Handling Application Block and Logging Application Block. The website uses Directory Services APIs to query for employee data stored in Active Directory, such as the employee's manager. The manager is the person who can approve the expenses.

The aExpense application implements the trusted subsystem to connect to SQL Server. It authenticates with a Windows domain account. The SQL database uses SQL Server authentication mode. The aExpense application stores its information on SQL Server. Scans of receipts are stored on a file share.

There are two background services, both implemented as Windows services. One periodically runs and generates thumbprints of the scanned receipts. It also compresses large images for increased storage efficiency. The other background service periodically queries the database for expenses that need to be reimbursed. It then generates a flat file that the payment system can process. This service also imports the payment results and sends them back to aExpense after the payments are made.

3

Getting to the Cloud

This chapter walks you through the first steps of migrating an application to Windows® Azure™ technology platform. You'll see an example of how to take an existing business application, developed using ASP.NET, and move it to the cloud. This first stage is only concerned with getting the application to work in the cloud without losing any functionality. It does address some "big" issues, such as security and data storage that are relevant to almost any cloud-based application.

This first stage doesn't explore how to improve the application by exploiting the features available on the Windows Azure platform. In addition, the on-premises version of the application that you'll see is not complete; it contains just enough basic functionality to get started. The following chapters discuss how to improve the application by using some of the features available on the Windows Azure platform, and you'll see more features added to the application. For now, you'll see how to take your first steps into the cloud.

The Premise

The existing aExpense application is a business expense submission and reimbursement system used by Adatum employees. The application is built with ASP.NET 3.5, deployed in Adatum's data center, and is accessible from the Adatum intranet. The application relies on the Microsoft Active Directory® directory service to authenticate employees. It also uses Active Directory to access some of the user profile data that the application requires, for example, an employee's cost center and manager. Because aExpense uses Windows authentication, it recognizes the credentials used when employees log on to the corporate network and doesn't need to prompt them again for their user names and passwords.

The aExpense access control rules use application-specific roles such as "Employee" and "Manager." Access control is intermixed with the application's business logic.

Integration with Active Directory really simplifies the task of managing this application. The aExpense application leverages Active Directory's access management facilities, and the cost center and manager information that Adatum store in Active Directory.

The aExpense application uses a simple SQL Server® database for storing application data, and the application uses LINQ to SQL as its data access mechanism. The application is configured to connect to SQL Server by using integrated security, and the website uses a service account to log on to the database.

The aExpense application uses the Enterprise Library Logging Application Block and the Exception Handling Application Block for logging diagnostic information from the application.

Figure 1 shows a whiteboard diagram of the structure of the on-premises aExpense application.

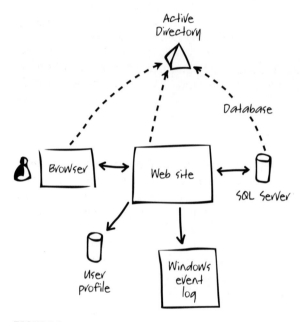

FIGURE 1
aExpense as an on-premises application

Goals and Requirements

◈ *Your decision to move an application to the cloud should be based on clear goals and requirements.*

In this first phase, Adatum has a number of goals for the migration of the aExpense application to the cloud that the team summarizes as "Getting it to work in the cloud." Optimizing the application for the cloud and exploiting the features of Windows Azure will come later.

Adatum identified some specific goals to focus on in this first phase. The aExpense application in the cloud must be able to access all the same data that the on-premises version of the application can access. This includes the business expense data that the application processes and the user profile data, such as a user's cost center and manager, that it needs to enforce the business rules in the application.

However, Adatum would like to remove any dependency on Active Directory from aExpense and avoid having the application call back into Adatum from the cloud.

A second goal is to make sure that operations staff have access to the same diagnostic information from the cloud-based version of aExpense as they have from the existing on-premises version of the application.

A significant concern that Adatum has about a cloud-based solution is security, so a third goal is to continue to control access to the aExpense application based on identities administered from within Adatum, and to enable users to access the application by using their existing credentials. Adatum does not want the overhead of managing additional security systems for its cloud-based applications.

Overall, the goals of this phase are to migrate aExpense to the cloud while preserving the user experience and the manageability of the application, and to make as few changes as possible to the existing application.

We want to avoid having to make any calls back into Adatum from the cloud application. This would add significantly to the complexity of the solution.

Overview of the Solution

The first step was to analyze the existing application to determine which pieces would need to change when it was migrated to the cloud. Remember that the goal at this stage is to make the application work in the cloud while making as few changes as possible to the application.

The migration project team determined that they could replace SQL Server with SQL Azure to meet the application's data storage requirements. They could easily copy the existing database structure and contents to SQL Azure.

At this stage, Adatum wants to make as few changes as possible to the application.

> **Note:** *You can use the SQL Azure Migration Wizard at http:// sqlazuremw.codeplex.com/ to help you to migrate your local SQL Server databases to SQL Azure.*

They also determined that the application could continue to use the Enterprise Library application blocks in Windows Azure, and that the cloud-based application could continue to generate the same diagnostic information as the on-premises version.

It would be great if we could continue to use tried and tested code in the cloud version of the application.

> **Note:** *You can download a white paper that explains the capabilities and limitations of Enterprise Library 5.0 when it is used by .NET applications designed to run on the Windows Azure platform from http://wag.codeplex.com/.*

The on-premises aExpense application stores users' preferred reimbursement methods by using the ASP.NET profiles feature. The default ASP.NET profile provider uses SQL Server as its storage mechanism. Because SQL Azure is a relatively expensive storage mechanism (compared to Windows Azure table storage), and because the profile data is very simple, the team decided to use a profile provider implementation that used Windows Azure table storage. Switching to a different profile provider should have no impact on any existing code in the application.

The biggest changes to the application that the team identified were in the authentication and authorization functionality. The Adatum team decided to modify the application to use a claims-based system. Adatum will configure an on-premises Active Directory Federation Services (ADFS) claims issuer in their data center. When a user tries to access the aExpense application in the cloud, that user will be redirected to this claims issuer. If the user has not already logged on to the Adatum domain, the user will provide his or her Windows credentials, and the claims issuer will generate a token that contains a set of claims obtained from Active Directory. These claims will include the user's role membership, cost center, and manager. This will minimize the changes needed in the application and remove the direct dependency that the current version of the application has on Active Directory because the application will obtain the required user data from the claims issuer (the claims issuer still has to get the data from Active Directory on behalf of the aExpense application). The external claims issuer can integrate with Active Directory, so that application users will continue to have the same single sign-on experience.

Figure 2 shows the whiteboard drawing that the team used to explain the architecture of aExpense would look like after the migration to Windows Azure.

Using claims can simplify the application by delegating responsibilities to the claims issuer.

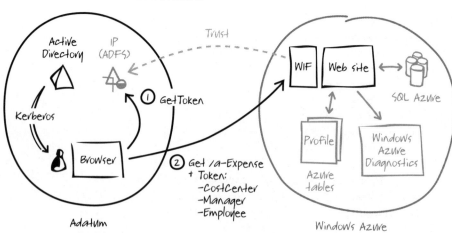

FIGURE 2
aExpense as an application hosted in Windows Azure

Inside the Implementation

Now is a good time to walk through the process of migrating aExpense into a cloud-based application in more detail. As you go through this section, you may want to download the Microsoft Visual Studio® development system solution from http://wag.codeplex.com/. This solution contains implementations of the aExpense application, before and after the migration. If you are not interested in the mechanics, you should skip to the next section.

◈ *Use the Visual Studio Cloud Service project template to get started with your cloud project.*

CREATING A WEB ROLE

The developers at Adatum created the Visual Studio solution for the cloud-based version of aExpense by using the Windows Azure Cloud Service template. This template generates the required service configuration and service definition files, and the files for the web and worker roles that the application will need.

Note: *For more information about how to create a Windows Azure Cloud Service project in Visual Studio, take a look at Appendix A.*

This first cloud-based version of aExpense has a single web role that contains all the code from the original on-premises version of the application.

The service definition file defines the endpoint for the web role. The aExpense application only has a single HTTPS endpoint, which requires a certificate. In this case, it is known as "localhost." When you deploy the application to Windows Azure, you'll also have to upload the certificate.

```
<ServiceDefinition name="aExpense.Azure" xmlns="…">
  <WebRole name="aExpense">
    <InputEndpoints>
      <InputEndpoint name="HttpsIn" protocol="https" port="443"
        certificate="localhost" />
    </InputEndpoints>
    <ConfigurationSettings>
      <Setting name="DiagnosticsConnectionString" />
      <Setting name="DataConnectionString" />
    </ConfigurationSettings>
    <Certificates>
      <Certificate name="localhost" storeLocation="LocalMachine"
        storeName="My" />
    </Certificates>
  </WebRole>
</ServiceDefinition>
```

Note: *For a discussion of certificate names when your cloud-based application has a custom DNS name, see Appendix D. The "local-host" certificate is only used for testing your application.*

The service configuration file defines the aExpense web role. It contains the connection strings that the role will use to access storage and details of the certificates used by the application. The application uses the **DataConnectionString** to connect to the Windows Azure storage holding the profile data, and uses the **DiagnosticsConnectionString** to connect to the Windows Azure storage for saving logging and performance data. The connection strings will need to change when you deploy the application to the cloud so that the application can use Windows Azure storage.

```xml
<ServiceConfiguration serviceName="aExpense.Azure" xmlns="…">
  <Role name="aExpense">
    <Instances count="1" />
    <ConfigurationSettings>
      <Setting name="DiagnosticsConnectionString"
               value="DefaultEndpointsProtocol=https;
               AccountName={Azure storage account name};
               AccountKey={Azure storage shared key}" />
      <Setting name="DataConnectionString"
               value="DefaultEndpointsProtocol=https;
               AccountName={Azure storage account name};
               AccountKey={Azure storage shared key}" />
    </ConfigurationSettings>
    <Certificates>
      <Certificate name="localhost" thumbprint="…"
                   thumbprintAlgorithm="sha1" />
    </Certificates>
  </Role>
</ServiceConfiguration>
```

In Chapter 5, you'll see how Adatum automated editing the configuration file and uploading the certificate as part of the automated deployment process.

Note: *The values of "Azure storage account name" and "Azure storage shared key" are specific to your Windows Azure storage account.*

SECURING AEXPENSE

Before the migration, aExpense used Windows Authentication to authenticate users. This is configured in the Web.config file of the application.

After the migration, the aExpense application delegates the process of validating credentials to an external claims issuer instead of using Windows Authentication. You make this configuration change in the Web.config file.

Note: *To find out more about claims-based Identity, the **FedUtil** tool, and Windows Identity Foundation (WIF), take a look at the book,* A Guide to Claims-Based Identity and Access Control. *You can download a .pdf copy of this book from http://msdn.microsoft.com/en-us/library/ff423674.aspx.*

The first thing that you'll notice in the Web.config file is that the authentication mode is set to **None**, while the requirement for all users to be authenticated has been left in place.

```
<authorization>
  <deny users="?" />
</authorization>
<authentication mode="None" />
```

You can make these changes to the Web.config file by running the **FedUtil** tool.

The **WSFederationAuthenticationModule** (FAM) and **Session AuthenticationModule** (SAM) modules now handle the authentication process. You can see how these modules are loaded in the **httpModules** section of the Web.config file.

```
<httpModules>
  …
  <add name="WSFederationAuthenticationModule"
       type="Microsoft.IdentityModel.Web.
           WSFederationAuthenticationModule, …" />
  <add name="SessionAuthenticationModule"
       type="Microsoft.IdentityModel.Web.
           SessionAuthenticationModule, …" />
</httpModules>
```

When the modules are loaded, they're inserted into the ASP.NET processing pipeline in order to redirect the unauthenticated requests to the claims issuer, handle the reply posted by the claims issuer, and transform the security token sent by the claims issuer into a **Claims Principal** object. The modules also set the value of the **HttpContext. User** property to the **ClaimsPrincipal** object so that the application has access to it.

More specifically, the **WSFederationAuthenticationModule** redirects the user to the issuer's logon page. It also parses and validates the security token that is posted back. This module also writes an encrypted cookie to avoid repeating the logon process. The **SessionAuthenticationModule** detects the logon cookie, decrypts it, and repopulates the **ClaimsPrincipal** object. After the claim issuer authenticates the user, the aExpense application can access the authenticated user's name.

The Web.config file contains a new section for the **Microsoft. IdentityModel** that initializes the Windows Identity Foundation (WIF) environment.

```
<microsoft.identityModel>
  <service>

    ...
  </service>
</microsoft.identityModel>
```

You can also use a standard control to handle the user logout process from the application. The following code example from the Site.Master file shows a part of the definition of the standard page header.

```
<div id="toolbar">
    Logged in as:
    <i>
      <%= AntiXss.HtmlEncode(this.Context.User.Identity.Name) %>
    </i> |
    <idfx:FederatedPassiveSignInStatus
          ID="FederatedPassiveSignInStatus1"
          runat="server"
          OnSignedOut="FederatedPassiveSignInStatus1SignedOut"
          SignOutText="Logout" FederatedPassiveSignOut="true"
          SignOutAction="FederatedPassiveSignOut" />
</div>
```

You'll also notice a small change in the way that aExpense handles authorization. Because the authentication mode is now set to **None** in the Web.config file, the authorization rules in the Web.config file now explicitly deny access to all users as well as allowing access for the designated role.

```
<location path="Approve.aspx">
  <system.web>
    <authorization>
      <allow roles="Manager" />
      <deny users="*"/>
    </authorization>
  </system.web>
</location>
```

The claim issuer now replaces the ASP.NET role management feature as the provider of role membership information to the application.

There is one further change to the application that potentially affects the authentication process. If you were to run the aExpense application on more than one web role instance in Windows Azure, the default cookie encryption mechanism (which uses DPAPI) is not appropriate because each instance has a different key. This would mean that a cookie created by one web role instance would not be readable by another web role instance. To solve this problem you should use a cookie encryption mechanism that uses a key shared by all the web role instances. The following code from the Global.asax file shows how to replace the default **SessionSecurityHandler** object and configure it to use the **RsaEncryptionCookieTransform** class.

> Although the initial deployment of aExpense to Windows Azure will only use a single web role, we need to make sure that it will continue to work correctly when we scale up the application. That is why we use RSA with a certificate to encrypt the session cookie.

```
private void OnServiceConfigurationCreated(object sender,
    ServiceConfigurationCreatedEventArgs e)
{
    List<CookieTransform> sessionTransforms =
        new List<CookieTransform>(
            new CookieTransform[]
            {
                new DeflateCookieTransform(),
                new RsaEncryptionCookieTransform(
                    e.ServiceConfiguration.ServiceCertificate),
                new RsaSignatureCookieTransform(
                    e.ServiceConfiguration.ServiceCertificate)
            });
    SessionSecurityTokenHandler sessionHandler =
    new
     SessionSecurityTokenHandler(sessionTransforms.AsReadOnly());

    e.ServiceConfiguration.SecurityTokenHandlers.AddOrReplace(
        sessionHandler);
}
```

MANAGING USER DATA

Before the migration, aExpense used an LDAP query to retrieve Cost Center, Manager, and Display Name information from Active Directory. It used the ASP.NET Role provider to retrieve the role membership of the user, and the ASP.NET Profile Provider to retrieve the application specific data for the application—in this case, the preferred reimbursement method. The following table summarizes how aExpense accesses user data, and where the data is stored before the migration:

User Data	Access Mechanism	Storage
Role Membership	ASP.NET Role Provider	SQL Server
Cost Center	LDAP	Active Directory
Manager	LDAP	Active Directory
Display Name	LDAP	Active Directory
User Name	ASP.NET Membership Provider	SQL Server
Preferred Reimbursement Method	ASP.NET Profile Provider	SQL Server

After the migration, aExpense continues to use the same user data, but it accesses the data differently. The following table summarizes how aExpense accesses user data, and where the data is stored after the migration:

User Data	Access Mechanism	Storage
Role Membership	Claim	Active Directory
Cost Center	Claim	Active Directory
Manager	Claim	Active Directory
Display Name	Claim	Active Directory
User Name	Claim	Active Directory
Preferred Reimbursement Method	ASP.NET Profile Provider	Windows Azure Table Storage

The external issuer delivers the claim data to the aExpense application after it authenticates the application user.

The external issuer delivers the claim data to the aExpense application after it authenticates the application user. The aExpense application uses the claim data for the duration of the session and does not need to store it.

The application can read the values of individual claims whenever it needs to access claim data. You can see how to do this if you look in the **ClaimHelper** class.

PROFILE DATA

Before the migration, aExpense used the ASP.NET profile feature to store application-specific user settings. Adatum tries to avoid customizing the schema in Active Directory, so aExpense stores a user's preferred reimbursement method by using the profile feature. The default Profile Provider stores the profile properties in a SQL Server database.

Using the profile feature makes it very easy for the application to store small amounts of user data. You enable the profile feature and specify the properties to store in the Web.config file.

```
<profile defaultProvider="SqlProvider">
  <providers>
    <clear />
    <add name="SqlProvider"
         type="System.Web.Profile.SqlProfileProvider"
         connectionStringName="aExpense"
         applicationName="aExpense" />
  </providers>
  <properties>
    <add name="PreferredReimbursementMethod" />
  </properties>
</profile>
```

We don't like to customize the Active Directory schema if we can possibly avoid it. Schema changes have far-reaching implications and are difficult to undo.

You can access a profile property value in code like this.

```
var profile = ProfileBase.Create(userName);
string prm =
    profile.GetProperty<string>("PreferredReimbursementMethod");
```

After migration, aExpense continues to use the profile system to store the preferred reimbursement method for each user. Although it is possible to use the SQL Server profile provider in Windows Azure by using the custom scripts at http://support.microsoft.com/kb/2006191/, the solution uses a sample provider that utilizes Windows Azure table storage to store profile information. You can download this provider from http://code.msdn.microsoft.com/windowsazuresamples. The only change required for the application to use a different profile provider is in the Web.config file.

Using a profile provider to access profile data minimizes the code changes in the application.

```
<profile defaultProvider="TableStorageProfileProvider">
  <providers>
    <clear />
    <add name="TableStorageProfileProvider"
         type="AExpense.Providers.TableStorageProfileProvider"
         applicationName="aExpense" />
  </providers>

  <properties>
    <add name="PreferredReimbursementMethod" />
  </properties>
</profile>
```

Using the **TableStorageProfileProvider** class does raise some issues for the application:

- The TableStorageProfileProvider is unsupported sample code.
- You must migrate your existing profile data from SQL Server to Windows Azure table storage.
- You need to consider whether, in the long run, Windows Azure table storage is suitable for storing profile data.

Even with these considerations to taken into account, using the table storage profile provider enabled Adatum to keep the changes in the application to a minimum; this means that the running costs of the application will be lower than they would be using SQL Azure.

> **Note:** *Chapter 4, "How Much Will It Cost?", describes the relative costs of using Windows Azure storage and SQL Azure.*
> *Chapter 5, "Phase 2: Automating Deployment and Using Windows Azure Storage," provides more information about using Windows Azure table storage.*

CONNECTING TO SQL SERVER

◈ *Connecting to SQL Azure instead of an on-premises SQL Server only requires a configuration change.*

Before the migration, aExpense stores application data in a SQL Server database. In this first phase, the team moved the database to SQL Azure and the data access code in the application remained unchanged. The only thing that needs to change is the connection string in the Web.config file.

```
<add name="aExpense" connectionString=
  "Data Source={Server Name};
  Initial Catalog=aExpense;
  UId={SQL Azure User Id};
  Pwd={SQL Azure User Password};
  Encrypt=True;
  TrustServerCertificate=False;"
  providerName="System.Data.SqlClient" />
```

> **Note:** *The values of **Server Name**, **SQL Azure User Id**, and **SQL Azure User Password** are specific to your SQL Azure account.*

There are two things to notice about the connection string. First, notice that because SQL Azure does not support Windows Authentication; the credentials for your SQL Azure account are stored in plain text. You should consider encrypting this section of the Web.config file. This will add to the complexity of your application, but it will enhance the security of your data. If your application is likely to run on multiple role instances, you must use an encryption mechanism that uses keys shared by all the role instances.

Note: *To learn how to encrypt configuration sections in your Web.config file, read the article, "How To: Encrypt Configuration Sections in ASP.NET 2.0 Using RSA," on MSDN® at http://msdn.microsoft.com/en-us/library/ms998283.aspx.*

The second thing to notice about the connection string is that it specifies that all communications with SQL Azure are encrypted. Even though your application may reside on a computer in the same data center as SQL Azure, you have to treat that connection as if it was using the internet.

SQL Azure Connection Timeout

When you try to connect to SQL Azure, you can specify a connection timeout value. If the timeout expires before establishing a connection, an error occurs, which your application must handle. How your application handles a timeout error depends on the specific circumstances, but possible strategies include keep retrying the connection until it succeeds, report the error to the user, or log the error and move on to another task.

The default connection timeout value is 15 seconds, but because the SQL Azure Service Level Agreement (SLA) specifies that an SLA violation does not occur until 30 seconds have elapsed, you should set your connection timeout to 30 seconds.

Note: *To retry connections you can use the **RetryPolicy** delegate in the **Microsoft.WindowsAzure.StorageClient** namespace. The article at http://blogs.msdn.com/windowsazurestorage/archive/2010/04/22/savechangeswithretries-and-batch-option.aspx describes how to use this delegate to retry saving changes to Windows Azure table storage, but you could adapt this approach to work with a context object in LINQ to SQL or ADO.NET Entity Framework.*

Handling Dropped Connections

If a connection to SQL Azure drops while your application is using the connection, you should immediately try to re-establish the connection. If possible, you should then retry the operation that was in progress before the connection dropped, or in the case of a transaction, retry the transaction. It is possible for a connection to fail between sending a message to commit a transaction and receiving a message that reports the outcome of the transaction. In this circumstance, you must have some way of checking whether the transaction completed successfully in order to determine whether you must retry it.

◈ *Any traffic within the data center is considered "internet," so it should be encrypted.*

You can also add protection to your SQL Azure database by configuring the SQL Azure firewall in the SQL Azure portal. You can use the SQL Azure firewall to specify the IP addresses of the computers that are permitted to connect to your SQL Azure server.

DIAGNOSTICS

The aExpense application uses the Logging Application Block and the Exception Handling Application Block from the Enterprise Library. The cloud-based version of aExpense continues to use these application blocks to help support and operations staff at Adatum troubleshoot problems. Although there are minimal changes required in the application to use these blocks in the cloud version of aExpense, the procedure for accessing the log files is different.

For aExpense to write logging information to Windows Azure logs, Adatum made a change to the Web.config file to make the Logging Application Block use the Windows Azure trace listener.

> The Logging Application Block and the Exception Handling Application Block are part of the Enterprise Library. We use them in a number of applications within Adatum.

> We want to have access to the same diagnostic data when we move to the cloud.

```
<listeners>
<add listenerDataType="Microsoft.Practices.EnterpriseLibrary.
  Logging.Configuration.SystemDiagnosticsTraceListenerData,
  Microsoft.Practices.EnterpriseLibrary.Logging, Ver-
sion=5.0.414.0,
  Culture=neutral, PublicKeyToken=31bf3856ad364e35"
  type="Microsoft.WindowsAzure.Diagnostics
.DiagnosticMonitorTraceListener,
  Microsoft.WindowsAzure.Diagnostics, Version=1.0.0.0,
Culture=neutral,
  PublicKeyToken=31bf3856ad364e35"
  traceOutputOptions="Timestamp, ProcessId"
  name="System Diagnostics Trace Listener" />
</listeners>
```

If you create a new Windows Azure Cloud Service project in Visual Studio, the Web.config file will contain the configuration for the Azure trace listener. The following code example from the Web.config file shows the trace listener configuration you must add if you are migrating an existing ASP.NET web application.

```
<system.diagnostics>
    <trace>
      <listeners>
        <add type="Microsoft.WindowsAzure.Diagnostics
.DiagnosticMonitorTraceListener,
            Microsoft.WindowsAzure.Diagnostics, Version=1.0.0.0,
            Culture=neutral, PublicKeyToken=31bf3856ad364e35"
            name="AzureDiagnostics">
          <filter type="" />
        </add>
      </listeners>
    </trace>
  </system.diagnostics>
```

By default in Windows Azure, diagnostic data is not automatically persisted to storage; instead, it is held in a memory buffer. In order to access the diagnostic data, you must to add some code to your application that transfers the data to Windows Azure storage. You can either schedule Windows Azure to transfer log data to storage at timed intervals, or perform this task on-demand.

Setup and Physical Deployment

When you're developing an application for Windows Azure, it's best to do as much development and testing as possible by using the local development fabric. When the application is ready, you can deploy it to Windows Azure for further testing. You shouldn't need to make any code changes before deploying to Windows Azure, but you will need to make sure that you upload any certificates that the application requires and update the configuration files for the Windows Azure environment.

> Because persisting diagnostic data to Windows Azure storage costs money, we will need to plan how long to keep the diagnostic data in Windows Azure and how we are going to download it for offline analysis.

> **Note:** *You can upload SSL certificates to Windows Azure by using the Windows Azure Developer Portal at http://windows.azure.com/ or by using a script. For information about how to upload certificates by using a Windows PowerShell™ command line script, see Chapter 5, "Phase 2: Automating Deployment and Using Windows Azure Storage."*

ROLE INSTANCES, UPGRADE DOMAINS, AND FAULT DOMAINS

Deploying multiple instances of web roles and worker roles is an easy way to scale out your application to meet increased demand. It's also easy to add or remove role instances as and when you need them, either through the Windows Azure Developer Portal or by using scripts, so you only pay for the services you actually need. You can also use multiple role instances to enable fault tolerant behavior in your application, and to add the ability to perform "live" upgrades of your application.

If you have two or more role instances, Windows Azure organizes them into virtual groupings known as upgrade domains. When you perform an in-place upgrade of your application, Windows Azure upgrades a single domain at a time; this ensures that the application remains available throughout the process. Windows Azure stops, upgrades, and restarts all the role instances in the upgrade domain before moving on to the next one.

◈ *Use multiple role instances to scale out your application, add fault tolerance, and enable in-place upgrades.*

Note: *There are some limitations to the types of upgrade that you can perform like this. In particular, you cannot modify the service configuration or add or remove roles from the application. You can also specify how many upgrade domains your application should have in the service configuration file.*

In Windows Azure, fault domains are a physical unit of failure. If you have two or more role instances, Windows Azure will allocate them to multiple fault domains, so that if one fault domain fails, there will still be running instances of your application. Windows Azure determines how many fault domains your application uses.

Windows Azure also ensures upgrade domains and fault domains are orthogonal, so that the role instances in an upgrade domain are spread across different fault domains.

DEPLOYMENT SCRIPTS

Manually modifying your application's configuration files before you deploy the application to Windows Azure is an error-prone exercise. The developers at Adatum have developed a set of deployment scripts that automatically update the configuration files, package the application files, and upload the application to Windows Azure. You'll see more of these scripts later.

USING A MOCK ISSUER

By default, the downloadable version of aExpense is set up to run on a standalone development workstation. This is similar to the way you might develop your own applications. It's generally easier to start with a single development computer.

Using a simple, developer-created claims issuer is good practice during development and unit testing.

To make this work, the developers of aExpense wrote a small stub implementation of an issuer. You can find this code in the downloadable Visual Studio solution. The project is in the Dependencies folder and is named Adatum.SimulatedIssuer.

When you first run the aExpense application, you'll find that it communicates with the stand-in issuer. The issuer issues predetermined claims.

It's not very difficult to write this type of component, and you can reuse the downloadable sample, or you can start with the template included in the Windows Identity Foundation (WIF) SDK.

Note: *You can download the WIF SDK from the Microsoft Download Center. The book,* A Guide to Claims-Based Identity and Access Control, *describes several ways you can create a claims issuer. You can download a PDF copy of this book from http://msdn.microsoft.com/en-us/library/ff423674.aspx.*

CONVERTING TO A PRODUCTION ISSUER

When you are ready to deploy to a production environment, you'll need to migrate from the simulated issuer that runs on your development workstation to a component such as ADFS 2.0.

Making this change requires two steps. First, you need to modify the Web application's Web.config file using the **FedUtil** utility such that it points to the production issuer. Next, you need to configure the issuer so that it recognizes requests from your Web application and provides the appropriate claims.

> **Note:** *To learn more about **FedUtil** and configuring applications to issue claims, take a look at the book, A Guide to Claims-Based Identity and Access Control. You can download a PDF copy of this book from http://msdn.microsoft.com/en-us/library/ff423674.aspx.*

You can refer to documentation provided by your production issuer for instructions about how to add a relying party and how to add claims rules.

When you forward a request to a claim issuer, you must include a *wreply* parameter that tells the claim issuer to return the claims. If you are testing your application locally and in the cloud, you don't want to hard code this URL because it must reflect the real address of the application. The following code shows how the aExpense application generates the *wreply* value dynamically in the Global.asax.cs file.

◈ *Building the wreply parameter dynamically simplifies testing the application in different environments.*

```
private void
  WSFederationAuthenticationModule_RedirectingToIdentityProvider
  (object sender, RedirectingToIdentityProviderEventArgs e)
{
    HttpRequest request = HttpContext.Current.Request;
    Uri requestUrl = request.Url;
    StringBuilder wreply = new StringBuilder();

    wreply.Append(requestUrl.Scheme); // e.g. "http" or "https"
    wreply.Append("://");
    wreply.Append(request.Headers["Host"] ??
        requestUrl.Authority);
    wreply.Append(request.ApplicationPath);

    if (!request.ApplicationPath.EndsWith("/"))
    {
        wreply.Append("/");
    }

    e.SignInRequestMessage.Reply = wreply.ToString();
}
```

ISOLATING ACTIVE DIRECTORY

The aExpense application uses Windows Authentication. Because developers do not control the identities in their company's enterprise directory, it is sometimes useful to swap out Active Directory with a stub during the development of your application.

The on-premises aExpense application (before the migration) shows an example of this. To use this technique, you need to make a small change to the Web.config file to swap Windows Authentication for Forms Authentication and then add a simulated LDAP profile store to the application. Swap Windows Authentication for Forms Authentication with the following change to the Web.config file.

```
<authentication mode="Forms">
  <forms name=".ASPXAUTH"
      loginUrl="~/SimulatedWindowsAuthentication.aspx"
      defaultUrl="~/default.aspx" requireSSL="true">
  </forms>
</authentication>
```

You need to add a logon page to the application that enables you to select the user that you want to use for testing. In aExpense, this page is known as SimulatedWindowsAuthentication.aspx.

You also need to add a class that simulates an LDAP lookup for the Active Directory attributes that your application needs. In this example, the **GetAttributes** method simulates the LDAP query "&(objectCategory=person)(objectClass=user);costCenter;manager; displayName".

```
public static class SimulatedLdapProfileStore
{
    public static Dictionary<string, string> GetAttributesFor(
        string userName, string[] attributes)
    {
        Dictionary<string, string> results;

        switch (userName)
        {
            case "ADATUM\\johndoe":
                results = new Dictionary<string, string>
                {
                    { "costCenter", "31023" },
                    { "manager", "ADATUM\\mary" },
                    { "displayName", "John Doe" }
                };
                break;
```

```
        ...
    }

    return results;
  }
}
```

Note: *These code samples come from the BeforeAzure solution
in the downloadable solutions.*

SQL SERVER

At this stage, the development team at Adatum is working with
sample data, so the deployment script builds a sample database in SQL
Azure (you can use the ResetSampleDatabaseInAzure.cmd script in
the Setup folder in the solution download if you need to manually
recreate the SQL Azure database). They will need to create a script
that transfers data from the on-premises version of SQL Server to
Windows Azure, when they come to migrate the live application. To
migrate an existing database schema to SQL Azure, you can use SQL
Server Management Studio to export the schema as a Transact-SQL
script, and then run the script against SQL Azure. To move data to
SQL Azure, you can use SQL Server Integration Service. However, the
team is planning to investigate whether they need SQL Azure at all,
or whether the application can utilize Windows Azure table storage.
Therefore, they haven't spent any time yet developing a data
migration strategy.

> **Note:** *You can get an overview of the limitations of SQL
> Azure that are important to be aware of at
> http://msdn.microsoft.com/en-us/library/ff394102.aspx.*

> **Note:** *You can get an overview of how to migrate a database
> to SQL Azure at http://msdn.microsoft.com/en-us/library/
> ee730904.aspx. You can also use the SQL Azure Migration
> Wizard at http://sqlazuremw.codeplex.com/ to help you to
> migrate your local SQL Server databases to SQL Azure*

ACCESSING DIAGNOSTICS LOG FILES

The on-premises version of aExpense uses the Logging Application
Block and the Exception Handling Application Block to capture
information from the application and write it to the Windows event
log. The Windows Azure version of the application continues to use
the same application blocks, and through a configuration change, it is
able to write log data to the Windows Azure logging system.

However, to access the log data in Windows Azure, you have to perform a few more steps. First, you need to save the log data to persistent storage. You can do this manually by using the Windows Azure Developer Portal, or you can add code your application to dump the log data to storage at scheduled intervals. Second, you need to have some way of viewing the log data in Windows Azure storage.

> **Note:** For details about some tools you can use to manage the log data when it has been persisted to Windows Azure storage, see Appendix E.

To access your log files in Windows Azure, you can find a utility that lets you access your Windows Azure storage remotely or develop some scripts that download them for you on a regular basis.

More Information

Appendix A of this guide provides a walkthrough of creating a new Windows Azure Cloud Service project in Visual Studio and a description of the files that this project template creates for you.

You can download the latest versions of Windows Azure Tools for Microsoft Visual Studio and the Windows Azure SDK from the Microsoft Download Center.

MSDN contains plenty of information about Windows Azure and SQL Azure. A good starting place is at http://msdn.microsoft.com/en-us/library/dd163896.aspx.

The Windows Azure Getting Started page (http://www.microsoft.com/windowsazure/getstarted) contains links to plenty of resources to help you learn about developing applications for Windows Azure.

4   How Much Will It Cost?

This chapter presents a basic cost model for running the aExpense application in the cloud. It makes some assumptions about the usage of the application and uses the current pricing information for Windows® Azure™ technology platform services to estimate annual operational costs.

The Premise

The existing, on-premises, version of aExpense is a typical business application. Adatum selected this application as a pilot cloud migration project because the application has features that are common to many of Adatum's other business applications, and a Adatum hopes that any lessons learned from the project can be applied elsewhere. Adatum has deployed the aExpense application in its data center, with components installed across several different servers. The web application is hosted on a Windows Server box that it shares with another application. aExpense also shares a SQL Server® database software installation with several other applications. aExpense has its own dedicated drive array for storing scanned expense receipts.

The current deployment of aExpense is sized for average use, not peak use, so during the busy two days at month-end when the majority of users submit their business expense claims, the application can be slow and unresponsive.

Goals and Requirements

It is difficult for Adatum to determine accurately how much it costs to run the current version of aExpense. The application uses several different servers, shares an installation of SQL Server with several other business applications, and is backed up as part of the overall backup strategy in the data center.

◈ *It is very difficult to estimate the operational costs of an existing on-premises application.*

Although Adatum cannot determine the existing running costs of the application, Adatum wants to estimate how much it will cost to run in the cloud. One of the specific goals of the pilot project is to discover how accurately it can predict running costs for cloud based applications.

A second goal is to estimate what cost savings might be possible by configuring the application in different ways. Adatum will then be able to assign a cost to a particular level of service, which will make it much easier to perform a cost-benefit analysis on the application. A specific example of this in the aExpense application is to estimate how much it will cost to deploy for peak demand at the busy month-end period.

Overall, Adatum would like to see greater transparency in managing the costs of its suite of business applications.

> You can manage the cost of a cloud-based application by changing its behavior through configuration changes.

Overview of the Solution

The first step was to analyze what Adatum will be billed for every month for a cloud-based version of aExpense. Figure 1 shows the services that Microsoft will bill Adatum for each month for the cloud version of the aExpense application.

> The simple cost model in this chapter does not include an estimate for the cost of any worker roles that Adatum may add to the aExpense application, and also assumes a single, small, web role instance. In addition, the model doesn't include any cost estimates for testing environments. Adatum should review its cost estimates when the aExpense application design is complete and when Adatum completes stress-testing the application.

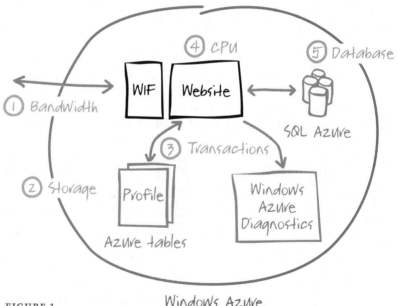

FIGURE 1
Billable services

The following table summarizes the current monthly rates in U.S. dollars for these services.

Service	Description	Cost
1. In/Out Bandwidth	This is the web traffic between the user's browser and the aExpense site.	In: $0.10/gigabyte (GB) Out: $0.15/GB
2. Windows Azure Storage	In aExpense, this will be used to store just profile data initially. Later, it will also store scanned receipt images.	$0.15/GB
3. Transactions	Each interaction with the storage system is billed.	$0.01/10 kilobyte (K) transactions
4. Compute	For the time the aExpense web roles are running.	Small size role $0.12/hour
5. SQL Storage	SQL Azure database.	Up to 1 GB: $9.99 Up to 10 GB: $99.99

> **Note:** *You can find the pricing for other regions at http://www.microsoft.com/WindowsAzure/offers/.*

BANDWIDTH COST ESTIMATE FOR AEXPENSE

aExpense is not a bandwidth intensive application. Assuming that all scanned receipt images will be transferred back and forth to the application twice, and taking into account the web traffic for the application, Adatum estimated that 4 GB of data would move each way every month.

Data transfer	GB/month	$/GB/month	Total/month
Inbound	4 GB	$0.10	$0.40
Outbound	4 GB	$0.15	$0.60
		Total/year	$12

WINDOWS AZURE STORAGE ESTIMATE FOR AEXPENSE

Based on an analysis of existing usage, on average 60 percent of 5,000 Adatum employees submit 10 business expense items per month. Each scanned receipt averages 15 KB in size, and to meet regulatory requirements, the application must store 7 years of history. This gives an estimated storage requirement for the application of 36 GB.

Storage		Cost	Total/month
GB stored/month	36 GB	$0.15/ GB	$5.40
Storage transactions/ month	90,000	$0.01/10 K	$0.09
		Total/year	$65.88

COMPUTE ESTIMATE FOR AEXPENSE

Adatum's assumption here is that the application will run 24 hours/day, 365 days/year.

Hours	$/hour	Number of instances	Total/year
8760	$0.12	2	$2,102.40

SQL AZURE STORAGE REQUIREMENTS ESTIMATE

Adatum estimates that each business expense record in the database will require 2 KB of storage. So based on the analysis of existing usage (on average 60 percent of 5,000 Adatum employees submit 10 business expense items per month) and the requirement to store data for 7 years, this gives an estimated storage requirement of 4.8 GB.

SQL storage size	$/month	Total/year
Up to 10 GB	$99.99	$1,199.88

Figure 2 shows a summary of the estimated annual running costs for the aExpense application running on Windows Azure.

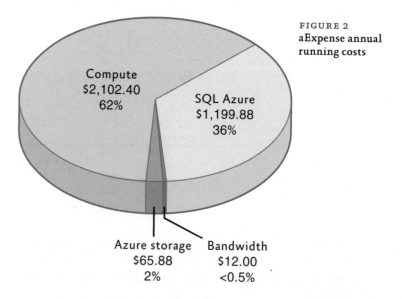

Compute
$2,102.40
62%

SQL Azure
$1,199.88
36%

Azure storage
$65.88
2%

Bandwidth
$12.00
<0.5%

Variations

One of the issues raised by users of the existing aExpense application is poor performance of the application during the two days at the end of the month when the application is most heavily used. To address this issue, Adatum then looked at the cost of doubling the compute capacity of the application for 2 days a month by adding an extra two web roles.

Hours/month	Hours/year	$/hour	Role instances	$/year
48	576	$0.12	2	$138.24

Adatum also examined the cost implications of limiting access to the application to 12 hours/day for only 6 days/week.

Compute	Number of role instances	Hours/day	Days/year	$/hour	$/year
Standard	2	12	313	$0.12	$901.44
Month End	2	12	24	$0.12	$69.12
				Total/year	$970.56

This is about 50 percent of the compute cost of running the application 24 hours/day, 365 days/year.

Adatum was also interested in comparing the cost of storing the business expense data in Windows Azure table storage instead of SQL Azure. The following table assumes that the storage requirement for seven years of data is the same 4.8 GB as for SQL Azure. It also assumes that each new business expense item is accessed 5 times during the month.

Storage		Cost	Total/Month
GB stored/month	4.8 GB	$0.15/ GB	$0.72
Storage transactions/month	150,000	$0.01/10 K	$0.15
		Total/year	$10.44

As you can see, this is a fraction of the cost of using SQL Azure ($1,199.88).

More Information

You can find the latest pricing information for Windows Azure at http://www.microsoft.com/windowsazure/pricing/.

Appendix D of this guide explains how you can use DNS with Windows Azure.

A common complaint about the existing version of aExpense is its poor performance at the time when most people want to use it.

It's easy to redirect users to an "Application is not currently available" page by using DNS.

5

PHASE 2

Automating Deployment and Using Table Storage

This chapter walks you through the changes Adatum made to the aExpense application during the second phase of the project. You'll see how Adatum extended the build process for aExpense to include a step that deploys the packaged application directly to Windows® Azure™ technology platform. You'll also see how Adatum changed the aExpense application to use Windows Azure table storage instead of SQL Azure and how the development team met some of the challenges they encountered along the way. The user-perceived functionality of the application didn't change from the previous phase.

The Premise

At the end of the first phase of the project, Adatum now had a version of the aExpense application that ran in the cloud. When the team at Adatum developed this version, they kept as much as possible of the original application, changing just what was necessary to make it work in Windows Azure.

The team does most of its testing against the local development fabric, which makes it easy for them to debug issues with the code. They also deploy the application to Windows Azure for additional testing in a staging environment in the cloud. They have found that manually deploying the application to Windows Azure through the Windows Azure Developer Portal was error-prone, especially editing the configuration files with the correct connection strings.

> **Note:** *Chapter 7, "Application Life Cycle Management for Windows Azure Applications," discusses testing applications for Windows Azure in more detail.*

A simple cost analysis of the existing solution has revealed that SQL Azure would account for about one third of the annual running costs of the application. Because the cost of using Windows Azure table storage is much lower than using SQL Azure, Adatum is keen to investigate whether it can use Windows Azure table storage instead.

Goals and Requirements

In this phase, Adatum has two specific goals. The first is to evaluate whether the aExpense application can use Windows Azure table storage instead of SQL Azure. Data integrity is critical, so Adatum wants to use transactions when a user submits multiple business expense items as a part of an expense submission.

The second goal is to automate the deployment process to Windows Azure. As the project moves forward, Adatum wants to be able to deploy versions of aExpense to Windows Azure without needing to manually edit the configuration files, or use the Windows Azure Developer Portal. This will make deploying to Windows Azure less error-prone, and easier to perform in an automated build environment.

Overview of the Solution

WCF Data Services was previously named ADO. NET Data Services.

Moving from SQL Azure to Windows Azure table storage involves some major changes to the application logic. The original version of aExpense used LINQ to SQL as the technology in the Data Access Layer (DAL) to communicate with SQL Azure. The DAL converted the data that it retrieved using LINQ to SQL to a set of domain-model objects that it passed to the user interface (UI). The new version of aExpense that uses Windows Azure table storage uses the .NET Client Library (which is a part of WCF Data Services) to interact with Windows Azure table storage.

> **Note:** *The Windows Azure table service only supports a subset of the functionality defined by the .NET Client Library for WCF Data Services. You can find more details at http://msdn.microsoft.com/en-us/library/dd894032.aspx.*

The business expense data is now organized into two Windows Azure tables that have a parent/child relationship: an expense header record and expense item detail records.

Figure 1 shows a whiteboard diagram of the structure of the Windows Azure tables.

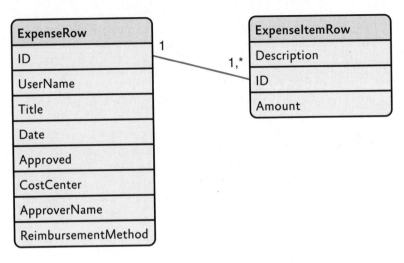

FIGURE 1
Windows Azure table structure

The developers at Adatum have updated the web UI of the aExpense application to support adding multiple business expense items as a part of an expenses submission. The aExpense application uses Entity Group Transactions to ensure the integrity of the data in the application.

The automated deployment of aExpense is handled in two stages. The first stage uses an MSBuild script to compile and package the application for deployment to Windows Azure. This build script uses a custom MSBuild task to edit the configuration files for a cloud deployment, instead of a local development fabric deployment. The second stage uses a PowerShell script with some custom CmdLets to perform the deployment to Windows Azure.

Inside the Implementation

Now is a good time to walk through these changes in more detail. As you go through this section, you may want to download the Microsoft® Visual Studio® development system solution from http://wag.codeplex.com/. This solution contains the implementation of aExpense, after the changes made in this phase. If you are not interested in the mechanics, you should skip to the next section.

AUTOMATING DEPLOYMENT TO WINDOWS AZURE
Although you should not have to make any code changes when you deploy to Windows Azure instead of the local development fabric, you will almost certainly need to make some configuration changes. The aExpense application now uses Windows Azure table storage for

◈ *Deploying to the cloud will require configuration changes for the application.*

storing business expense data, so you must change both the **DataConnectionString** and the **DiagnosticsConnectionString** in the ServiceConfiguration.csfg file to provide the information for the Windows Azure storage account that you want to use.

This is what the relevant section of the configuration file looks like when the application is using development storage.

```
<ConfigurationSettings>
  <Setting name="DiagnosticsConnectionString"
    value="UseDevelopmentStorage=true" />
  <Setting name="DataConnectionString"
    value="UseDevelopmentStorage=true" />
</ConfigurationSettings>
```

This is what it looks like when the application is using cloud storage.

```
<ConfigurationSettings>
  <Setting name="DiagnosticsConnectionString"
    value="DefaultEndpointsProtocol=https;
    AccountName={Azure storage account name};
    AccountKey={Azure storage shared key}" />
  <Setting name="DataConnectionString"
    value="DefaultEndpointsProtocol=https;
    AccountName={Azure storage account name};
    AccountKey={Azure storage shared key}" />
</ConfigurationSettings>
```

Note: *The values of **Azure storage account name** and **Azure storage shared key** are specific to your Windows Azure storage account.*

Note: *If you want to edit these settings manually, you should use the tools in Visual Studio instead of directly editing the XML.*

The MSBuild script for the aExpense application uses a custom build task named RegexReplace to make the changes during the build. The example shown here replaces the development storage connection strings with the Windows Azure storage connection strings.

```
<Target Name="SetConnectionStrings"
DependsOnTargets="BuildTasks">
  <RegexReplace
    Pattern='Setting name="DiagnosticsConnectionString"
      value="UseDevelopmentStorage=true"'
    Replacement='Setting name="DiagnosticsConnectionString"
      value="DefaultEndpointsProtocol=https;
      AccountName=$(StorageAccountName);
```

You should also have a target that resets the development connection strings for local testing.

```
      AccountKey=$(StorageAccountKey)"'
    Files='SourceCode\
Azure-SqlAzure\aExpense.Azure\ServiceConfiguration.cscfg'/>
  <RegexReplace
    Pattern='Setting name="DataConnectionString"
      value="UseDevelopmentStorage=true"'
    Replacement='Setting name="DataConnectionString"
      value="DefaultEndpointsProtocol=https;
      AccountName=$(StorageAccountName);
      AccountKey=$(StorageAccountKey)"'
    Files='SourceCode\
Azure-SqlAzure\aExpense.Azure\ServiceConfiguration.cscfg'/>
</Target>
```

Note: *The source code for the RegexReplace custom build task is available in the download for this phase.*

The team at Adatum then developed a PowerShell script that would deploy the packaged application to Windows Azure. You can invoke this script from an MSBuild task. This script uses the Windows Azure Service Management CmdLets, a library of PowerShell CmdLets that wrap the Windows Azure Service Management API and Diagnostics API. You can download this library at http://code.msdn.microsoft.com/azurecmdlets.

```
$cert = Get-Item cert:\CurrentUser\My\{Account API Certificate}
$sub = "{Account Subscription ID}"
$buildPath = $args[0]
$packagename = $args[1]
$serviceconfig = $args[2]
$servicename = $args[3]
$package = join-path $buildPath $packageName
$config = join-path $buildPath $serviceconfig
$a = Get-Date
$buildLabel = $a.ToShortDateString() + "-" + $a.ToShort-
TimeString()

if ((Get-PSSnapin | ?{$_.Name -eq "AzureManagementToolsSnapIn"})
-eq $null)
{
  Add-PSSnapin AzureManagementToolsSnapIn
}


$hostedService = Get-HostedService $servicename -Certificate $cert
-SubscriptionId $sub | Get-Deployment -Slot Staging
```

```
if ($hostedService.Status -ne $null)
{

    $hostedService |
      Set-DeploymentStatus 'Suspended' |
      Get-OperationStatus -WaitToComplete
    $hostedService |
      Remove-Deployment |
      Get-OperationStatus -WaitToComplete
}


Get-HostedService $servicename -Certificate $cert -SubscriptionId
$sub |
    New-Deployment Staging -package $package -configuration $config
-label $buildLabel -serviceName $servicename |
    Get-OperationStatus -WaitToComplete


Get-HostedService $servicename -Certificate $cert -SubscriptionId
$sub |
    Get-Deployment -Slot Staging |
    Set-DeploymentStatus 'Running' |
    Get-OperationStatus -WaitToComplete
```

The script needs the following two pieces of information to connect
to Windows Azure, and you should replace the values of **Account API
Certificate** and **Account Subscription ID** with values that are specific to your Windows Azure account:

- The thumbprint of the API certificate that is installed
  on your local computer. This certificate must match a
  certificate that you have uploaded to the Windows
  Azure Developer Portal on the Account page. For more
  information, see Appendix B.
- You can find your Subscription ID on the Account page
  in the Windows Azure Portal.

Note: *The API Certificate gives you access to all the Windows
Azure Service Management API functionality. You may want to
restrict access to this script to ensure that only authorized users
have access to your Windows Azure services. This is not the same
certificate as the SSL certificate used by the HTTPS endpoint.*

The deployment script takes four parameters:

- *buildPath.* This parameter identifies the folder where
  you build your deployment package. For example:
  C:\AExpenseBuildPath.

- *packagename*. This parameter identifies the package to upload to Windows Azure. For example: aExpense.Azure.cspkg.
- *serviceconfig*. This parameter identifies the service configuration file for your project. For example: ServiceConfiguration.cscfg.
- *servicename*. This parameter specifies the name of your Windows Azure hosted service. For example: aExpense.

The script first verifies that the Windows Azure Service Management CmdLets are loaded. Then, if there is an existing service, the script suspends and removes it. The script then deploys and starts the new version of the service.

MSBuild can invoke the PowerShell script in a task and pass all the necessary parameter values:

The examples here deploy aExpense to the staging environment. You can easily modify the scripts to deploy to production. You can also script in-place upgrades when you have multiple role instances.

```
<Target Name="Deploy"
  DependsOnTargets="BuildTasks;SetConnectionStrings;Build">
  <MSBuild
    Projects="SourceCode\
Azure-SqlAzure\aExpense.Azure\aExpense.Azure.ccproj"
    Targets="CorePublish"
    Properties="Configuration=$(BuildType)"/>

  <Exec WorkingDirectory="$(MSBuildProjectDirectory)"
    Command="C:\Windows\system32\WindowsPowerShell\v1.0\
powershell.exe -f
    deploy.ps1 $(PackageLocation) $(PackageName)
    $(ServiceConfigName) $(AccountName)" />

</Target>
```

Note: *On a 64-bit computer, because the targets file for Windows Azure is in the Program Files (x86) folder, you must run the 32-bit version of MSBuild and install the Windows Azure Service Management CmdLets for the 32-bit version of PowerShell. See Appendix C for details of how to build and install a 32-bit version of the CmdLets on a 64-bit computer.*

The aExpense application uses an HTTPS endpoint, so as part of the automatic deployment, Adatum needed to upload the necessary certificate. The following deploycert.ps1 PowerShell script performs this operation.

```
$cert = Get-Item cert:\CurrentUser\My\{Account API Certificate}
$sub = "{Account Subscription ID}"
$servicename = $args[0]
$certToDeploy = $args[1]
$certPassword = $args[2]

if ((Get-PSSnapin |
    ?{$_.Name -eq "AzureManagementToolsSnapIn"}) -eq $null)
{
   Add-PSSnapin AzureManagementToolsSnapIn
}

Add-Certificate -ServiceName $servicename -Certificate $cert
   -SubscriptionId $sub -CertificateToDeploy $certToDeploy
   -Password $certPassword
```

The script needs the following two pieces of information to connect to Windows Azure, and you should replace the values of **Account API Certificate** and **Account Subscription ID** with values that are specific to your Windows Azure account:

- The thumbprint of the API certificate installed on your local computer. This certificate must match a certificate that you have uploaded to the Windows Azure Portal on the Account page. For more information, see Appendix B.
- You can find your Subscription ID on the Account page in the Windows Azure Portal.

You must also pass the script three parameters:

- *servicename*. This parameter specifies the name of your Windows Azure service. For example: aExpense.
- *certToDeploy*. This parameter specifies the full path to the .pfx file that contains the certificate.
- *certPassword*. This parameter specifies the password that protects the private key in the .pfx file.

Note: *For information about how to generate a self-signed certificate to test your application using HTTPS, see Appendix F.*

Note: *The script doesn't check whether the certificate has already been deployed. If it has, the script will complete without an error.*

An MSBuild file can invoke this script and pass the necessary parameters. The following code is an example target from an MSBuild file.

```
<Target Name="DeployCert">
  <Exec WorkingDirectory="$(MSBuildProjectDirectory)"
    Command=
      "$(windir)\system32\WindowsPowerShell\v1.0\powershell.exe
      -f deploycert.ps1 $(HostedServiceName) $(CertLocation)
      $(CertPassword)" />
</Target>
```

STORING BUSINESS EXPENSE DATA IN WINDOWS AZURE TABLE STORAGE

Modifying the aExpense application to use Windows Azure table storage instead of SQL Azure meant that the developers at Adatum had to re-implement the Data Access Layer in the application. Because Windows Azure table storage uses a fundamentally different approach to storage, this was not simply a case of replacing LINQ to SQL with the .NET Client Library.

How Many Tables?

The most important thing to understand when transitioning to Windows Azure table storage is that the storage model is different from what you may be used to. In the relational world, the obvious data model for aExpense would have two tables, one for expense header entities, and one for expense detail entities, with a foreign-key constraint to enforce data integrity. The best data model to use is not so obvious with Windows Azure table storage for a number of reasons:

Use the .NET Client Library to access Windows Azure table storage.

- You can store multiple entity types in a single table in Windows Azure.
- Entity Group Transactions are limited to a single partition in a single table (partitions are discussed in more detail later in this chapter).
- Windows Azure table storage is relatively cheap, so you shouldn't be so concerned about normalizing your data and eliminating data redundancy.

Adatum could have used a single table to store both the expense header and expense detail entities. This approach would have enabled Adatum to use Entity Group Transactions to save an expense header entity and its related detail entities to a single partition in a single, atomic transaction. However, storing multiple entity types in the same table adds to the complexity of the application.

You have to stop thinking in relational terms when you are dealing with Windows Azure table storage.

Note: *You can find a description of how to store multiple entity types in the same table in the document at http://go.microsoft.com/fwlink/?LinkId=153401. Look at section 8.3.3, "Different Entity Kinds in the Same Table."*

Adatum decided on a two-table solution for aExpense with tables named Expense and ExpenseItem. You can see the table definitions in the **ExpenseRow** and **ExpenseItemRow** classes in the **AExpense. DataAccessLayer** namespace. This approach avoids the complexity of multiple entity types in a table, but it does make it more difficult to guarantee the integrity of the data because the expense header entity can't be saved in the same transaction as the expense detail entities. How Adatum solved this problem is described in the section, "Transactions in aExpense," later in this chapter.

> **Note:** *Adatum had to make a change to the data type that the application uses to store the business expense amount. In SQL Azure, this field was stored as a decimal. This data type is not supported in Windows Azure table storage and the amount is now stored as a double.*

> Choosing the right partition key is the most important decision you make that affects the performance of your storage solution.

◈ *The partition key and row key together make up a tuple that uniquely identifies any entity in table storage.*

Partition Keys and Row Keys

The second important decision about table storage is the selection of keys to use. Windows Azure table storage uses two keys: a partition key and a row key. Windows Azure uses the partition key to implement load balancing across storage nodes. The load balancer can identify "hot" partitions (partitions that contain data that is accessed more frequently than the data in other partitions) and run them on separate storage nodes in order to improve performance. This has deep implications for your data model design and your choice of partition keys:

> Each entry in a table is simply a property bag. Each property bag can represent a different entity type; this means that a single partition can hold multiple entities of the same or different types.

- The partition key forms the first part of the tuple that uniquely identifies an entity in table storage.
- You can only use Entity Group Transactions on entities in the same table and in the same partition. You may want to choose a partition key based on the transactional requirements of your application. Don't forget that a table can store multiple entity types.
- You can optimize queries based on your knowledge of partition keys. For example, if you know that all the entities you want to retrieve are located on the same partition, you can include the partition key in the where block of the query. If the entities you want to retrieve span multiple partitions, you can split your query into multiple queries and execute them in parallel across the different partitions.

Note: *If you want to create parallel queries, you should plan to use Parallel LINQ (PLINQ) instead of creating your own threads in the web role.*

The row key is a unique identifier for an entity within a partition and forms the second part of the tuple that uniquely identifies an entity in table storage.

In the aExpense application, Adatum decided to use the **UserName** property as the partition key of the Expense table. They anticipate that the vast majority of queries will filter based on the **UserName** property. For example, the website displays the expense submissions that belong to the logged on user. The ExpenseItem table uses the same partition key. This means that when a user inserts several ExpenseItem entities at the same time, the application can use a transaction to ensure that it inserts all the ExpenseItems (or none of them). It also means that all the data that belongs to a user is located on the same partition, so you only need to scan a single partition to retrieve a user's data.

Although the Expense and ExpenseItem tables use the same partition key values, you cannot have a transaction that spans tables in Windows Azure table storage.

Note: *In Chapter 8, "Phase 4: Adding More Tasks and Tuning the Application," this choice of partition key and row key is re-evaluated in the light of some results from testing the aExpense application.*

For the Expense table, the application uses a GUID as the row key to guarantee a unique value. Because Windows Azure tables do not support foreign keys, for the ExpenseItem table, the row key is a concatenation of the parent Expense entity's row key and a GUID for the ExpenseItem row. This enables the application to filter ExpenseItems by ExpenseID as if there was a foreign key relationship. The following code in the **SaveChanges** method in the **ExpenseRepository** class shows how the application creates this row key value from the **Id** property of the expense header entity and the **Id** property of the expense detail entity.

```
expenseItemRow.RowKey = string.Format(
    CultureInfo.InvariantCulture,
    "{0}_{1}", expense.Id, expenseItemRow.Id);
```

The following code example shows how to query for ExpenseItems based on ExpenseID.

A more natural way of writing this query would be to use **StartsWith** instead of **CompareTo**. However, **StartsWith** is not supported by the Windows Azure table service. You also get performance benefits from this query because the *where* clause includes the partition key.

```
char charAfterSeparator =
    Convert.ToChar((Convert.ToInt32('_') + 1));
var nextId = expenseId.ToString() + charAfterSeparator;

var expenseItemQuery =
    (from expenseItem in context.ExpenseItem
     where
     expenseItem.RowKey.CompareTo(expenseId.ToString()) >= 0 &&
     expenseItem.RowKey.CompareTo(nextId) < 0 &&
     expenseItem.PartitionKey.CompareTo(expenseRow.PartitionKey)
        == 0
     select expenseItem).AsTableServiceQuery();
```

Windows Azure places some restrictions on the characters that you can use in partition and row keys. Generally speaking, the restricted characters are ones that are meaningful in a URL. For more information, see http://msdn.microsoft.com/en-us/library/dd179338.aspx. In the aExpense application, it's possible that these illegal characters could appear in the **UserName** used as the partition key value for the Expense table.

> **Note:** *If there is an illegal character in your partition key, Windows Azure will return a Bad Request (400) message.*

To avoid this problem, the aExpense application encodes the **UserName** value using a base64 encoding scheme before using the **UserName** value as a row key. Implementing base64 encoding and decoding is very easy.

```
public static string EncodePartitionAndRowKey(string key)
{
    if (key == null)
    {
        return null;
    }


    return Convert.ToBase64String(
        System.Text.Encoding.UTF8.GetBytes(key));
}

public static string DecodePartitionAndRowKey(string encodedKey)
{
    if (encodedKey == null)
    {
        return null;
    }
```

```
    return System.Text.Encoding.UTF8.GetString(
        Convert.FromBase64String(encodedKey));
}
```

The team at Adatum first tried to use the **UrlEncode** method because it would have produced a more human readable encoding, but this approach failed because it does not encode the percent sign (%) character.

> **Note:** *According to the documentation, the percent sign character is not an illegal character in a key, but Adatum's testing showed that entities with a percent sign character in the key could not be deleted.*

Another approach would be to implement a custom escaping technique.

A custom method to transform the user name to a legal character sequence could leave the keys human-readable, which would be useful during debugging or troubleshooting.

Query Performance

As mentioned earlier, the choice of partition key can have a big impact on the performance of the application. This is because the Windows Azure load balancer tracks activity at the partition level, and can automatically migrate a busy partition to a separate storage node in order to improve data access performance for the application.

You can also use partition keys to improve the performance of individual queries. The current version of the application retrieves stored business expense submissions for a user by using this query.

```
var query = (from expense in context.Expenses
             where expense.UserName.CompareTo(userName) == 0
             select expense).AsTableServiceQuery();
```

As it stands, this query must scan all the partitions of the table to search for matching records. This is inefficient if there are a large number of records to search, and its performance may be further affected if it has to scan data across multiple storage nodes sequentially.

When Adatum stress tests the application, it plans to evaluate whether modifying the query to reference the partition key in the **where** block provides any significant performance improvements in the aExpense application.

It's important to understand the impact that partitions can have on query performance.

```
var query = (from expense in context.Expenses
             where expense.PartitionKey.CompareTo(
                 EncodePartitionAndRowKey(userName)) == 0
             select expense).AsTableServiceQuery();
```

Note: *If a table query does not include the partition key in its where clause, to avoid the potential performance problems associated with scanning multiple partitions, you should re-evaluate your choice of row key and partition key for the table.*

Transactions in aExpense

Figure 2 shows what happens when a user makes a business expense submission. The operation creates an expense master record and at least one expense detail item.

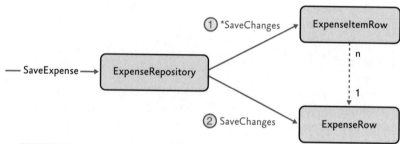

FIGURE 2
Saving a business expense submission

Adatum decided to store the Expense and ExpenseItem entities in two separate Windows Azure tables, but this means it cannot wrap the complete **SaveExpense** operation in a single transaction to guarantee its data integrity. The following code shows the hybrid solution that Adatum adopted that uses both a transaction and compensating code to ensure data integrity.

◈ *Transactions cannot span tables in Windows Azure table storage.*

```
public void SaveExpense(Expense expense)
{
    ExpenseDataContext context = new
        ExpenseDataContext(this.account);
    ExpenseRow expenseRow = expense.ToTableEntity();

    foreach (var expenseItem in expense.Details)
    {
        var expenseItemRow = expenseItem.ToTableEntity();
        expenseItemRow.PartitionKey = expenseRow.PartitionKey;
        expenseItemRow.RowKey =
            string.Format(CultureInfo.InvariantCulture,
            "{0}_{1}", expense.Id, expenseItemRow.Id);
        context.AddObject(ExpenseDataContext.ExpenseItemTable,
            expenseItemRow);
    }
```

```
context.SaveChanges(SaveChangesOptions.Batch);

context.AddObject(ExpenseDataContext.ExpenseTable,
    expenseRow);
context.SaveChanges();
}
```

Note: *The code sample does not include any retry logic for when the call to the **SaveChanges** method fails. The article at http://blogs.msdn.com/windowsazurestorage/archive/2010/04/22/ savechangeswithretries-and-batch-option.aspx summarizes how to use the **RetryPolicy** delegate to handle retry logic: when and how often to retry, which errors indicate not to retry. It also describes a workaround for a problem with retry policies and transactions.*

The transaction takes place (implicitly) in the Windows Azure table storage service. In the method, the code first adds multiple **Expenseltem** entities to the context and then calls the **SaveChanges** method. The **SaveChanges** method has a parameter **SaveChangesOptions. Batch** that tells the context to submit all the pending changes in a single request. If all the changes in the batch are to entities in the same partition of the same table, Windows Azure automatically uses an Entity Group Transaction when it persists the changes to table storage. An Entity Group Transaction provides the standard "all or nothing" transactional behavior to the operation.

At the moment, we're assuming that no one will submit more than 100 business expense items as part of a single submission. We need to add some additional validation to this code to ensure the **SaveChanges** method can use an Entity Group Transaction.

Note: *There are some additional restrictions on performing Entity Group Transactions: each entity can appear only once in the transaction, there must be no more than 100 entities in the transaction, and the total size of the request payload must not exceed 4 megabytes (MB).*

After the **Expenseltem** detail entities are inserted, the code saves the **ExpenseRow** header entity. The reason for saving the details first, followed by the header record, is that if there is a failure while saving the details, there will be no orphaned header record that could be displayed in the UI.

To resolve the potential issue of orphaned detail records after a failure, Adatum is planning to implement an "orphan collector" process that will regularly scan the Expense table looking for, and deleting, orphaned Expenseltem records.

Working with Development Storage

There are some differences between development table storage and Windows Azure table storage documented at http://msdn.microsoft.com/en-us/library/dd320275.aspx. The team at Adatum encountered the error "One of the request inputs is not valid" that occurs when testing the application with empty tables in development storage. The solution that Adatum adopted was to insert, and then delete, a dummy row into the Windows Azure tables if the application is running in the development fabric. During the initialization of the web role, the application calls the **CreateTableIfNotExist<T>** extension method in the **TableStorageExtensionMethods** class to check whether it is running against local development storage, and if this is the case, it adds, and then deletes, a dummy record to the application's Windows Azure tables.

The following code from the **TableStorageExtensionMethods** class demonstrates how the aExpense application determines whether it is using development storage and how it adds and deletes a dummy record to the table.

Don't assume that local development storage will work in exactly the same way as Windows Azure storage.

You should consider adding dummy records to all tables in local development storage.

```
public static bool CreateTableIfNotExist<T>(
    this CloudTableClient tableStorage, string entityName)
    where T : TableServiceEntity, new()
{

    bool result = tableStorage.CreateTableIfNotExist(entityName);

    // Execute conditionally for development storage only
    if (tableStorage.BaseUri.IsLoopback)
    {
        InitializeTableSchemaFromEntity(tableStorage,
            entityName, new T());
    }
    return result;
}

private static void InitializeTableSchemaFromEntity(
    CloudTableClient tableStorage, string entityName,
    TableServiceEntity entity)
{

    TableServiceContext context =
        tableStorage.GetDataServiceContext();
    DateTime now = DateTime.UtcNow;
    entity.PartitionKey = Guid.NewGuid().ToString();
    entity.RowKey = Guid.NewGuid().ToString();
```

```
Array.ForEach(
    entity.GetType().GetProperties(BindingFlags.Public |
    BindingFlags.Instance),
    p =>
    {
        if ((p.Name != "PartitionKey") &&
            (p.Name != "RowKey") && (p.Name != "Timestamp"))
        {
            if (p.PropertyType == typeof(string))
            {
                p.SetValue(entity, Guid.NewGuid().ToString(),
                    null);
            }
            else if (p.PropertyType == typeof(DateTime))
            {
                p.SetValue(entity, now, null);
            }
        }
    });

    context.AddObject(entityName, entity);
    context.SaveChangesWithRetries();
    context.DeleteObject(entity);
    context.SaveChangesWithRetries();
}
```

Retrieving Data from Table Storage

The aExpense application uses LINQ to specify what data to retrieve data from table storage. The following code example shows how the application retrieves expense submissions for approval by approver name.

◈ *Use the **AsTableService Query** method to return data from Windows Azure table storage.*

```
var query = (from expense in context.Expenses
    where expense.ApproverName.CompareTo(approverName) == 0
    select expense).AsTableServiceQuery();
```

The **AsTableServiceQuery** method converts the standard **IQueryable** result to a **CloudTableQuery** result. Using a **CloudTableQuery** object offers the following benefits to the application:

- Data can be retrieved from the table in multiple segments instead of getting it all in one go. This is useful when dealing with a large set of data.
- You can specify a retry policy for cases when the query fails.

Materializing Entities

In the aExpense application, all the methods in the **Expense Repository** class that return data from queries call the **ToList** method before returning the results to the caller.

```
public IEnumerable<Expense>
        GetExpensesForApproval(string approverName)
{

    ExpenseDataContext context = new
        ExpenseDataContext(this.account);


    var query = (from expense in context.Expenses

where expense.ApproverName.CompareTo(approverName) == 0
                select expense).AsTableServiceQuery();

    try
    {
        return query.Execute().Select(e => e.ToModel()).ToList();
    }
    catch (InvalidOperationException)
    {
        Log.Write(EventKind.Error,
          "By calling ToList(), this exception can be handled
           inside the repository.");
        throw;
    }
}
```

The reason for this is that calling the **Execute** method does not materialize the entities. Materialization does not happen until someone calls **MoveNext** on the **IEnumerable** collection. Without **ToList**, the first call to **MoveNext** happens outside the repository. The advantage of having the first call to the **MoveNext** method inside the **ExpenseRepository** class is that you can handle any data access exceptions inside the repository.

More Information

Appendix B of this guide gives you more information about working with the Windows Azure Service Management API.

Appendix C of this guide describes how to build the Windows Azure Service Management CmdLets for the 32-bit version of Power-Shell on a 64-bit computer.

You can download the latest versions of Windows Azure Tools for Microsoft Visual Studio and the Windows Azure SDK from the Microsoft Download Center.

MSDN® contains plenty of information about Windows Azure Table Storage. A good starting place is at http://msdn.microsoft.com/en-us/library/dd179423.aspx.

The Windows Azure Table document at http://go.microsoft.com/fwlink/?LinkId=153401 contains detailed information about working with Windows Azure table storage.

6

Uploading Images
and
Adding a Worker Role

This chapter walks you through the changes in the cloud-based version aExpense application that Adatum made when they added support for uploading, storing, and displaying scanned images of receipts. You'll see how the application uses Windows® Azure™ technology platform blob storage to store the image data, how the application uses a worker role in Windows Azure to perform background processing tasks on the images, and how the application uses shared access signatures to control access to the images. The chapter also introduces a simple set of abstractions that wrap a worker role in the expectation that the aExpense application will be given additional background tasks to perform in the future.

The Premise

During this phase of the project, the team at Adatum turned their attention to the first of the background processes in the aExpense application that performs some processing on the scanned images of business expense receipts that users upload.

The on-premises web application enables users to upload images of their business expense receipts and the application assigns a unique name to each image file before it saves the image to a file share. It then stores the path to the image in the SQL Server® database that holds the business expenses data. The application can then later retrieve the image related to an expense submission and display it through the user interface (UI).

The existing on-premises application also has a background process that processes the images, which is implemented as a Windows service. This process performs two tasks: first, it compresses the images to preserve disk space, and second, it generates a thumbnail image. By default, the application's UI displays the thumbnail, but if a user wants to see a more detailed image, it enables viewing the full-sized version of the image.

Goals and Requirements

Adatum has a number of goals for the implementation of the image-processing component of the application. Firstly, it wants to minimize the storage requirements for the images while maintaining the legibility of the information on the receipts.

It also wants to maintain the responsiveness of the application and minimize the bandwidth required by the UI. A user shouldn't have to wait after uploading an image while any necessary processing takes place, and the application should display image thumbnails with an option to display a full-sized version.

Finally, Adatum wants to maintain the privacy of its employees by making receipts visible only to the employee who submitted them and to the people responsible for approving the expense submission.

Overview of the Solution

The team at Adatum several significant changes to the implementation of the aExpense application for the Windows Azure–based version in this phase. The first decision to make was to select a storage mechanism for the scanned receipt images. A simple approach to the application's storage requirements would be to use the Windows Azure drive. This would have required minimal changes to the code from the on-premises version, because the Windows Azure drive is a simple NTFS volume that you can access by using the standard .NET I/O classes. The big drawback of this approach is that you can only write the Windows Azure drive from one role instance at a time. Adatum expect to deploy multiple instances of the aExpense web role to ensure high availability and scalability for the application. The approach adopted by Adatum was to store the image data in Windows Azure block blob storage; although this approach required more changes to the code, it was compatible with using multiple role instances.

Adatum decided to implement the image processing service by using a worker role in the cloud-based version. Most of the code from the existing on-premises version of the application that compressed images and generated thumbnails was simply repackaged in the worker role. Using a worker role to process the images offloads work from the application's web role and helps to improve the responsiveness of the UI by performing the image processing on a background thread. What did change was the way that the image processing service identified when it had a new image to process. Figure 1 shows how, in the on-premises version, the Windows Service uses the **FileSystem Watcher** class to generate an event whenever the application saves a new image to the file share. The aExpense application then invokes the image processing logic from the **OnCreated** event handler.

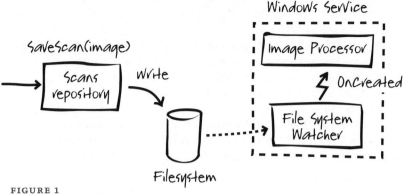

FIGURE 1
On-premises image processing

Adatum should review the cost estimates for the aExpense application now that the application includes a worker role.

For the cloud-based version of the application using blob storage, this approach won't work because there is no Windows Azure equivalent of the **FileSystemWatcher** class for blob storage. Instead, as Figure 2 shows, Adatum decided to use a Windows Azure queue.

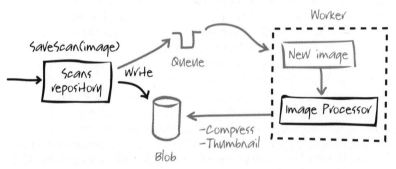

FIGURE 2
Cloud-based image processing

We can use a Windows Azure queue to communicate from the web role to the worker role.

Whenever a user uploads a new image to aExpense as part of an expense submission, the application writes a message to the queue and saves the image to blob storage. The worker role will pick up messages from the queue, compress the image, and then generate a thumbnail. After the worker role completes the image processing, it updates the expense item entity in Windows Azure table storage to include references to the image and the thumbnail and deletes the original image.

To display images in the UI, the application locates the images in blob storage from the information maintained in the expense item entity.

With Windows Azure queues, it is possible that a message could be read twice, either by two different worker roles, or by the same

With Windows Azure
queues, it is possible that
a message could be read
twice, either by two
different worker roles,
or by the same worker
role.

worker role. Although this would mean some unnecessary processing if it did occur, provided that the operation processing the message is idempotent, this would not affect the integrity of the application's data. In the aExpense application, a duplicate message causes the worker role to resize the original image and to generate the thumbnail a second time, overwriting the saved compressed image and thumbnail.

If your message processing method is not idempotent, there are several strategies that you can adopt to stop the message recipient processing a message multiple times:

- When you read a message from a queue, you can use the *visibilitytimeout* parameter to set how long the messages should be hidden from other readers (the default value is v30 seconds). This gives you time to make sure that you can process and delete the message from the queue before another client reads it. Getting a message from a queue does not automatically delete it from the queue. It is still possible for the *visibilitytimeout* period to expire before you delete the message, for example, if the method processing the message fails.

- Each message has a **DequeueCount** property that records how many times the message has been retrieved from the queue. However, if you rely on this property, and only process messages that have a **DequeueCount** value of **0**, your application must guard against the possibility that a message has been dequeued but not processed.

- You could also add a unique transaction identifier to the message and then save the identifier in the blob's metadata properties. If, when you retrieve a message from a queue, the unique identifier in the message matches the unique identifier in the blob's metadata, you know that the message has already been processed once.

The application also allows users to view only images of receipts that they previously uploaded or images that belong to business expense submissions that they can approve. The application keeps other images hidden to protect other users' privacy. To achieve this, Adatum decided to use the Shared Access Signatures (SAS) feature in Windows Azure after they had evaluated a several other approaches.

In Windows Azure, all storage mechanisms can be configured to allow data to be read from anywhere by using anonymous requests, which makes the model shown in Figure 3 very easy to implement:

We evaluated three alternative approaches to making business expense receipt images browsable before deciding on shared access signatures.

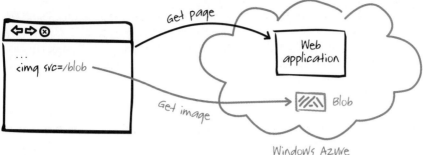

FIGURE 3
Directly addressable storage

In this scenario, you can access blob content directly through a URL like **https://<application>.blob.core.windows.net/<containername>/<blobname>**. In the aExpense application, you could save the URLs as part of the expense entities in Windows Azure table storage. This is not an appropriate approach for the aExpense application because it would make it easy for someone to guess the address of a stored image, although this approach would work well for data that you did want to make publicly available, such as logos, branding, or downloadable brochures. The advantages of this approach are its simplicity, the fact that data is cacheable, that it offloads work from the web server, and that it could leverage the Content Delivery Network (CDN) infrastructure in Windows Azure. The disadvantage is the lack of any security.

> **Note:** *Using deliberately obscure and complex URLs is a possible option, but this approach offers only weak protection and is not recommended.*

The second approach considered by Adatum for accessing receipt images in blob storage was to route the request through the web site in much the same way that a "traditional" tiered application routes requests for data through the middle tier. Figure 4 shows this model.

CDN enables you to cache blob data at strategically placed locations for delivering the content to users with the maximum available bandwidth.

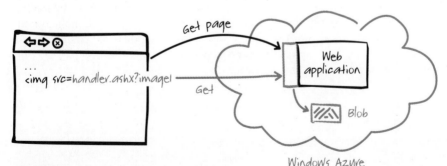

FIGURE 4
Routing image requests through the web server

In this scenario, there is no public access to the blob container, and the web application holds the access keys for blob storage. This is how aExpense writes the image data to blob storage. Although this approach would enable Adatum to control access to the images, it would add to the complexity of the web application and to the workload of the web server. A possible implementation of this scenario would be to use an HTTP handler to intercept image requests, check the access rules, and return the data. In addition, you couldn't use this approach if you wanted to use the Windows Azure CDN feature.

The approach that Adatum decided on for the aExpense application was to use the Windows Azure SAS feature. SAS enables you to control access to individual blobs, even though access is set at the container level, by generating blob access URLs that are only valid for a limited period of time. In the aExpense application, the web role generates these special URLs and embeds them in the page served to users. These special URLs then allow direct access to the blob for a limited period of time. There is some additional work for the web server, because it must generate the SAS URLs, but Windows Azure blob storage handles most of the work. The approach is reasonably secure because the SAS URLs, in addition to having a limited lifetime, also contain a uniquely generated signature, which makes it very difficult for anyone to guess a URL before it expires.

Inside the Implementation

Now is a good time to walk through these changes in more detail. As you go through this section, you may want to download the Microsoft® Visual Studio® development system solution from http://wag. codeplex.com/. This solution contains the implementation of aExpense after the changes in this phase are made. If you are not interested in the mechanics, you should skip to the next section.

UPLOADING AND SAVING IMAGES

In the aExpense application, the web role is responsible for uploading the image from the user's workstation and saving the initial, uncompressed version of the image. The following code in the **SaveExpense** method in the **ExpenseRepository** class saves the original, uncompressed image to blob storage.

```
this.receiptStorage.AddReceipt(expenseItem.Id.ToString(),
    expenseItem.Receipt, string.Empty);
```

The following code from the **ExpenseReceiptStorage** class shows how the application saves the image data to blob storage.

```
public string AddReceipt(string receiptId, byte[] receipt,
    string contentType)
{
    CloudBlob blob = this.container.GetBlobReference(receiptId);
    blob.Properties.ContentType = contentType;
    blob.UploadByteArray(receipt);

    return blob.Uri.ToString();
}
```

ABSTRACTING THE WORKER ROLE

Figure 5 summarizes the common pattern for the interaction between web roles and worker roles in Windows Azure.

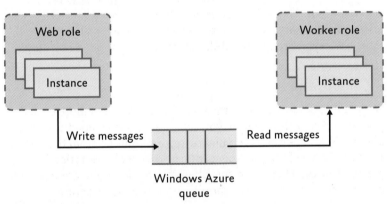

This is a very common pattern for communicating between the web role and the worker role.

FIGURE 5
Web-to-worker role communication with a Windows Azure queue

In this pattern, to communicate with the worker role, a web role instance places messages on to a queue, and a worker role instance polls the queue for new messages, retrieves them, and processes them. There are a couple of important things to know about the way the queue service works in Windows Azure. First, you reference a queue by name, and multiple role instances can share a single queue. Second, there is no concept of a typed message; you construct a message from either a string or a byte array. An individual message can be no more than 8 kilobytes (KB) in size.

Note: *If the size of your messages could be close to the maximum, be aware that Windows Azure converts all messages to Base64 before it adds them to the queue.*

In addition, Windows Azure implements an "at-least-once" delivery mechanism; thus, it does not guarantee to deliver messages on a first-in, first-out basis, or to deliver only a single copy of a message, so your application should handle these possibilities.

Although in the current phase of the migration of aExpense to Windows Azure, the worker role only performs a single task, Adatum expects the worker role to take on additional responsibilities in later phases. Therefore, the team at Adatum developed some simple "plumbing" code to hide some of the complexities of Windows Azure worker roles and Windows Azure queues and to make them easier to work with in the future. Figure 6 is a high-level description of these abstractions and shows where to plug in your custom worker role functionality.

◈ *Windows Azure does not guarantee to deliver messages on a first-in, first-out basis, or to deliver only a single copy of a message.*

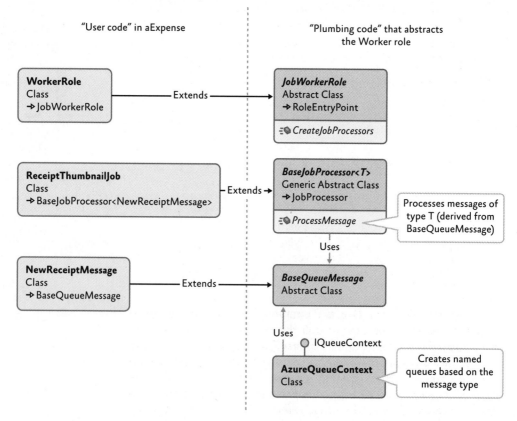

FIGURE 6
Relationship of "user code" to plumbing code

The "user code" classes are the ones that you will implement for each worker role and job type. The "plumbing code" classes are the reusable elements. The "plumbing code" classes are packaged in the **AExpense.Jobs**, **AExpense.Queues**, and **AExpense.QueueMessages** namespaces. The following two sections first discuss the "user code" and then the "plumbing code."

"User Code" in the aExpense Application

The code you'll see described in this section implements the job that will compress images and generate thumbnails in the worker role for the aExpense application. What you should see in this section is how easy it is to define a new job type for the worker role to perform. This code uses the "plumbing code" that the following section describes in detail.

For any new background task, you only need to implement the "user code" components.

The following code shows how the application initializes the worker role using the "plumbing code": you create a new class that derives from the **JobWorkerRole** and override the **CreateJob Processors** method. In this method, you instantiate your job processing objects that implement the **IJobProcessor** interface. As you can see, this approach makes it easy to plug in any additional job types that implement the **IJobProcessor** interface.

```
public class WorkerRole : JobWorkerRole
{
    protected override IEnumerable<IJobProcessor>
       CreateJobProcessors()
    {
       return new IJobProcessor[] { new receiptThumbnailJob() };
    }
}
```

> **Note:** *This code does not match exactly what you'll find in the downloaded solution because Adatum changed this code in the subsequent phase of this project. For more information, see Chapter 8, "Phase 4: Adding More Tasks and Tuning the Application."*

The constructor for the **ReceiptThumbnailJob** class specifies the interval the worker role uses to poll the queue and instantiates an **AzureQueueContext** object, an **ExpenseReceiptStorage** object, and an **ExpenseRepository** object for the worker role to use. The "plumbing code" passes a **NewReceiptMessage** object that contains the details of the image to process to the **ProcessMessage** method. This method then compresses the image referenced by the message and generates a thumbnail. The following code shows the constructor and the **ProcessMessage** method in the **ReceiptThumbnailJob** class.

```
public ReceiptThumbnailJob()
    : base(2000, new AzureQueueContext())
{
    this.receiptStorage = new ExpenseReceiptStorage();
    this.expenses = new ExpenseRepository();
}

public override bool ProcessMessage(NewReceiptMessage message)
{
    …
}
```

In the aExpense application, to send a message containing details of a new receipt image to the worker role, the web role creates a **New ReceiptMessage** object and calls the **AddMessage** method of the **AzureQueueContext** class. The following code shows the definition on the **NewReceiptMessage** class.

```
[DataContract]
public class NewReceiptMessage : BaseQueueMessage
{
    [DataMember]
    public string ExpenseItemId { get; set; }
}
```

> **Note:** It's important to use the **DataContract** and **DataMember** attributes in your message class because the **DataQueueContext** class serializes message instances to the JSON format.

The following code shows how the web role in aExpense puts a message onto the queue.

```
var queue = new AzureQueueContext(this.account);
queue.AddMessage(new NewReceiptMessage
    { ExpenseItemId = expenseItem.Id.ToString() });
```

The "Plumbing Code" Classes

Adatum developed these abstractions to simplify the way that you send messages from a web role to a worker role and to simplify the way that you code a worker role. The idea is that you can put a typed message onto a queue, and when the worker role retrieves the message, it routes it to the correct job processor for that message type. The previous section described a job processor in the aExpense application that processes scanned receipt images and that uses these abstractions. The following core elements make up these "plumbing code" classes:

> *The "plumbing code" classes simplify the way that you send messages from a web role to a worker role and the way that you implement a worker role.*

- A wrapper for the standard Windows Azure worker role's **RoleEntryPoint** class that abstracts the worker role's life cycle and threading behavior.
- A customizable job processor that enables users of the "plumbing code" classes to define their own job types for the worker role.
- A wrapper for the standard Windows Azure **CloudQueue** class that implements typed messages to enable message routing within the **JobWorkerRole** class.

Figure 7 summarizes how the "plumbing code" classes handle messages derived from the **BaseQueueMessage** class.

> Adatum expect to implement additional background processes, so it makes sense to create this "plumbing code."

FIGURE 7
Worker role "plumbing code" elements

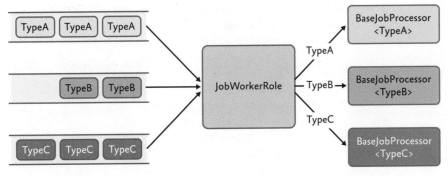

The message types that the "plumbing code" classes handle (like the **NewReceiptMessage** type in aExpense) are derived from the **Base QueueMessage** class shown in the following code example.

```
[DataContract]
public abstract class BaseQueueMessage
{
    private object context;

    public object GetContext()
    {
        return this.context;
    }

    public void SetContext(object value)
    {
        this.context = value;
    }
}
```

The "plumbing code" classes use the **AzureQueueContext** class to deliver messages to the worker role. The **AzureQueueContext** class creates named queues based on the message types, one queue for each message type that was registered with it. The following code shows the **Add** method in the **AzureQueueContext** class that you use to add a new message to a queue and the **ResolveQueueName** method that figures out the name of the queue to use.

```
public void AddMessage(BaseQueueMessage message)
{
    var queueName = ResolveQueueName(message.GetType());
    this.EnsureQueueExists(queueName);

    var json = Serialize(message.GetType(), message);
    var queue = this.queue.GetQueueReference(queueName);
    queue.AddMessage(new CloudQueueMessage(json));
}

public static string ResolveQueueName(MemberInfo messageType)
{
    return messageType.Name.ToLowerInvariant();
}
```

There are two other details to point out in the **AddMessage** method implementation. First, the "plumbing code" serializes messages to the JSON format, which typically produces smaller message sizes than an XML encoding (but possibly larger than a binary encoding).

Second, the **EnsureQueueExists** method calls the **CreateIfNotExist** method of the Windows Azure **CloudQueue** class. Calling the **CreateIfNotExist** method counts as a storage transaction and will add to your application's running costs.

> **Note:** *Microsoft currently bills you for storage transactions at $0.01/10 K. If you have high volumes of messages, you should check how frequently your application calls this method.*
>
> *In Chapter 8, "Phase 4: Adding More Tasks and Tuning the Application," the place where the application calls the* **CreateIfNotExist** *is revaluated following the results from performance testing on the application.*

If you are concerned about the running costs of the application, you should be aware of which calls in your code are chargeable!

The "plumbing code" classes deliver messages to job processor components, where a job processor handles a specific message type. The "plumbing code" classes include an interface named **IJob Processor** that defines two void methods named **Run** and **Stop** for starting and stopping a processor. The abstract **BaseJobProcessor** and **JobProcessor** classes implement this interface. In the aExpense application, the **ReceiptThumbnailJob** class that you've already seen extends the **BaseJobProcessor** class. The following code example shows how the **JobProcessor** class implements the **IJobProcessor** interface.

```csharp
private bool keepRunning;

public void Stop()
{
    this.keepRunning = false;
}

public void Run()
{
    this.keepRunning = true;
    while (this.keepRunning)
    {
        Thread.Sleep(this.SleepInterval);
        this.RunCore();
    }
}

protected abstract void RunCore();
```

The following code example shows how the **BaseJobProcessor** class provides an implementation of the **RunCore** method.

```
protected bool RetrieveMultiple { get; set; }
protected int RetrieveMultipleMaxMessages { get; set; }

protected override void RunCore()
{
    if (this.RetrieveMultiple)
    {
        var messages = this.Queue.GetMultipleMessages<T>
            (this.RetrieveMultipleMaxMessages);
        if (messages != null)
        {
            foreach (var message in messages)
            {
                this.ProcessMessageCore(message);
            }
        }
        else
        {
            this.OnEmptyQueue();
        }
    }
    else
    {
        var message = this.Queue.GetMessage<T>();
        if (message != null)
        {
            this.ProcessMessageCore(message);
        }
        else
        {
            this.OnEmptyQueue();
        }
    }
}
```

As you can see, the **RunCore** method can retrieve multiple messages from the queue in one go. The advantage of this approach is that one call to the **GetMessages** method of the Windows Azure **CloudQueue** class only counts as a single storage transaction, regardless of the number of messages it retrieves. The code example also shows how the **BaseJobProcessor** class calls the generic **GetMessage** and

GetMultipleMessages of the **AzureQueueContext** class specifying the message type by using a generic type parameter.

The following code example shows how the **BaseJobProcessor** constructor assigns the job's polling interval and the **AzureQueue-Context** reference.

```
protected BaseJobProcessor(int sleepInterval,
    IQueueContext queue) : base(sleepInterval)
{
    if (queue == null)
    {
        throw new ArgumentNullException("queue");
    }

    this.Queue = queue;
}
```

The remaining significant methods in the **BaseJobProcessor** class are the **ProcessMessageCore** and the abstract **ProcessMessage** methods shown below.

```
protected int MessagesProcessed { get; set; }

private void ProcessMessageCore(T message)
{
    var processed = this.ProcessMessage(message);
    if (processed)
    {
        this.Queue.DeleteMessage(message);
        this.MessagesProcessed++;
    }
}

public abstract bool ProcessMessage(T message);
```

It's cheaper and more efficient to retrieve multiple messages in one go if you can. However, these benefits must be balanced against the fact that it will take longer to process multiple messages; this risks the messages becoming visible to other queue readers before you delete them.

The **Run** method invokes the **ProcessMessageCore** method when it finds new messages to process. The **ProcessMessageCore** method then calls the "user-supplied" implementation of the **ProcessMessage** method before it deletes the message from the queue. In the aExpense application, this implementation is in the **ReceiptThumbnailJob** class.

The final component of the "plumbing code" is the abstract **JobWorkerRole** class that wraps the standard Windows Azure **RoleEntryPoint** class for the worker role. The following code example shows the **Run** method in this class.

```
protected IEnumerable<IJobProcessor> Processors { get; set; }

protected abstract IEnumerable<IJobProcessor>
    CreateJobProcessors();

public override void Run()
{
    this.Processors = this.CreateJobProcessors();

    var threads = new List<Thread>();

    foreach (var processor in this.Processors)
    {
        var t = new Thread(processor.Run);
        t.Start();
        threads.Add(t);
    }

    foreach (var thread in threads)
    {
        thread.Join();
    }
}
```

You need to keep the worker role alive!

The **Run** method invokes the abstract **CreateProcessors** method that is implemented in "user code." In the aExpense application, you can find this implementation in the **WorkerRole** class. The **Run** method then creates a new thread for each job processor and then waits for all the threads to finish.

PROCESSING THE IMAGES

The following code example shows how the aExpense application implements the image processing functionality in the **Process Message** method in the **ReceiptThumbnailJob** class.

```
public override bool ProcessMessage(NewReceiptMessage message)
{
    var expenseItemId = message.ExpenseItemId;
    var imageName = expenseItemId + ".jpg";

    byte[] originalPhoto =
        this.receiptStorage.GetReceipt(expenseItemId);

    if (originalPhoto != null && originalPhoto.Length > 0)
    {
```

```
    var thumb = ResizeImage(originalPhoto, ThumbnailSize);
    var thumbUri =
        this.receiptStorage.AddReceipt(Path.Combine(
        "thumbnails", imageName), thumb, "image/jpeg");

    var photo = ResizeImage(originalPhoto, PhotoSize);
    var photoUri = this.receiptStorage.AddReceipt(imageName,
        photo, "image/jpeg");

    this.expenses.UpdateExpenseItemImages(expenseItemId,
        photoUri, thumbUri);

    this.receiptStorage.DeleteReceipt(expenseItemId);

    return true;
    }

    return false;
}
```

This method retrieves the image name from the message sent to the worker role, and then it creates two new versions of the image, one a thumbnail, and one a "standard" size. It then deletes the original image. The method can process images in any standard format, but it always saves images as JPEGs.

Although we limit uses to uploading images that are less than 1,024 KB in size, in order to save space we decided not to store the original images. We found that resizing to a standard size provided acceptable quality.

> **Note:** *The **ProcessMessage** method should be idempotent, so there are no unwanted side effects if a message is delivered multiple times. The **ProcessMessage** method should also contain some logic to handle "poison" messages that cannot be processed for some reason.*

MAKING THE IMAGES AVAILABLE USING SHARED ACCESS SIGNATURES

To make images of receipts viewable in the UI, the team at Adatum used Shared Access Signatures (SAS) to generate short-lived, secure URLs to address the images in blob storage. This approach avoids having to give public access to the blob container and minimizes the amount of work that the web server has to perform because the client can access the image directly from blob storage.

The following code example shows how the application generates the SAS URLs in the **GetItemByID** method in the **ExpenseRepository** class by appending the SAS to the blob URL. The aExpense application uses an HTTPS endpoint, so the blob reference and signature elements of the blob's URL are protected by SSL from "man-in-the-middle" attacks.

◈ *The aExpense application uses Shared Access Signatures to provide limited access to blobs in private containers.*

Note: *Using SSL ensures that all URL data except for the
hostname is encrypted.*

```
CloudBlob receiptBlob =
    container.GetBlobReference(item.ReceiptUrl.ToString());
item.ReceiptUrl = new Uri(item.ReceiptUrl.AbsoluteUri +
    receiptBlob.GetSharedAccessSignature(policy));
```

The **GetSharedAccessSignature** method takes **SharedAccessPolicy**
object as a parameter. This policy specifies the access permissions and
the lifetime of the generated URL. The following code shows the
policy that the aExpense application uses, granting read permission
for one minute to an image. The application generates a new SAS
whenever a user tries to access an expense submission.

```
private readonly TimeSpan sharedSignatureValiditySpan;

var policy = new SharedAccessPolicy
{
    Permissions = SharedAccessPermissions.Read,
    SharedAccessExpiryTime = DateTime.UtcNow +
        this.sharedSignatureValiditySpan
};
```

Note: *The application does not specify a value for the **Shared
AccessStartTime** property of the **SharedAccessPolicy** object.
Setting this value to the current time can cause problems if there
is a clock skew between the client and the server and you try to
access the blob immediately.*

  *As long as the **Get** request for a blob starts before the expiry
time, the request will succeed, even if the response streaming
continues past the expiration time. As a part of the logical **Get**
operation, if your application chooses to retry on a **Get** failure,
which is the default StorageClient library policy, any retry request
made after the expiration time will fail. If you decide to have a
short validity period for the URL, make sure that you issue a single
Get request for the entire blob and use a custom retry policy so
that when you retry the request, you get a new SAS for the URL.*

More Information

You can download the latest versions of Windows Azure Tools for Microsoft Visual Studio and the Windows Azure SDK from the Microsoft Download Center.

MSDN® contains plenty of information about Windows Azure Blob Storage. A good starting place is at http://msdn.microsoft.com/en-us/library/dd135733.aspx.

To find out more about controlling access to Azure storage, including shared access signatures, look at http://msdn.microsoft.com/en-us/library/ee393343.aspx.

You can find a summary of the Windows Azure service architecture at http://msdn.microsoft.com/en-us/library/dd179341.aspx.

7

Application Life Cycle Management

This chapter outlines an application life cycle management approach for Windows® Azure™ technology platform applications. Although specific requirements will vary between applications and across organizations, everyone develops applications, then tests them, and finally deploys them. This chapter focuses on where applications should be tested, and how the deployment process should be managed to make sure that only authorized personnel have access to the live production environment.

The Premise

Adatum have a well-defined set of processes for deploying applications to their on-premises servers. They use separate servers for testing, staging, and production. When the development team releases a new version of the application, its progression through the testing, staging, and production servers is tightly controlled. Very rarely, though, small fixes, such as updating the text on an ASPX page, are applied directly to the production servers.

Goals and Requirements

Adatum has a number of goals for application life cycle management for Windows Azure. Adatum wants to have a clearly defined process for deploying applications to Windows Azure, with clearly defined roles and responsibilities. More specifically, it wants to make sure that access to the live environment is only available to a few key people, and that any changes to the live environment are traceable.

In addition, Adatum wants to be able to roll back the live environment to a previous version if things go wrong. In a worst-case scenario, they would like to be able to pull the application back to be an on-premises application.

> ◈ *You should have a clearly defined process for deploying applications to Windows Azure.*

Adatum would like to perform some testing on an application in an environment that is as similar as possible to the live environment.

Finally, Adatum would like to minimize the costs of maintaining all the required environments and be able to identify the costs of running the development and test environments separately from the live production environment.

Overview of the Solution

Adatum can use the local development fabric and storage for all development tasks and for a great deal of testing before it deploys anything to Windows Azure. However, Adatum must test its applications in the cloud before it deploys them to the live production environment.

> All Windows Azure environments in the cloud are the same; there's nothing special about a test or staging area. However, there are differences between the local development fabric and the cloud fabric, which is why it's important to test your application in the cloud.

To achieve this goal, Adatum has two Windows Azure subscriptions. One is an account used for testing, and one is the live production account. Because each account has its own Windows Live® ID, and its own set of API keys, Adatum can limit access to each environment to a particular set of personnel. Members of the testing team and key members of the development team have access to the testing account. Only two key people in the Adatum operations department have access to the production account.

◈ *Don't forget that any time you do something in Windows Azure, even if it's only testing it costs money.*

Both of these accounts are standard Windows Azure accounts, and because they are identical environments, Adatum can be confident that application code will run in the same way on both of them. Adatum can also be sure that application deployment will work in the same way in both environments because it can use the same package to deploy to both test and production.

Adatum can also perform some testing by running the application on the development fabric, but pointing the application at storage in the test Windows Azure environment. This is important because there are more differences between development storage and cloud storage than between the development fabric and the cloud runtime environment. Also, cloud storage is relatively cheap to use as compared to other cloud resources.

> In Windows Azure, you can be sure that different accounts have identical environments—this is something that's very difficult to guarantee in your on-premises environments.

Microsoft bills Adatum separately for the two environments, which makes it easy for Adatum to separate the running costs for the live environment, from the costs associated with development and test. This allows Adatum to manage the product development budget separately from the operational budget, in a manner similar to the way it manages budgets for on-premises applications.

Setup and Physical Deployment

Figure 1 summarizes the application life cycle management approach at Adatum.

Because development and testing staff don't have access to the production storage account keys, there's no risk of accidentally testing on live data.

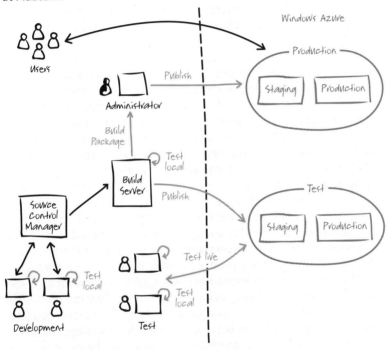

FIGURE 1
Adatum's application life cycle management environment

The preceding diagram shows the two separate Windows Azure environments that Adatum uses for test and production, as well as the on-premises environment that consists of development computers, test computers, a build server, and a source code management tool.

WINDOWS AZURE ENVIRONMENTS

There are two ways to access a Windows Azure environment to per-form configuration and deployment tasks. The first is through the Windows Azure Developer Portal, where a single Windows Live ID has access to everything in the portal. The second is by using the Windows Azure Service Management API, where API certificates are used to access to all the functionality exposed by the API. In both cases, there is currently no way to restrict users to only be able to manage a subset of the available functionality, for example to only be able to manage the storage aspects of the account. Within Adatum, almost all operations that affect the test or production environment are performed using scripts instead of the Developer portal.

> **Note:** *For information about the Windows Azure Service Management API, see Chapter 5, "Phase 2: Automating Deployment and Using Windows Azure Storage," of this guide.*

Within Adatum, only key developers and key members of the testing team have access to the test Windows Azure environment. Only two people in the operations department have access to the production Windows Azure environment.

The Windows Live ID and API certificates used to access the test environment are different from the ones used to access the produc-tion system.

Production and Staging Areas

In Windows Azure, you can deploy an application to either a staging or a production area. A common scenario is to deploy first to the stag-ing area and then, at the appropriate time, move the new version to the production area. The two areas are identical environments; the only difference is in the URL you use to access them. In the staging area, the URL will be something obscure like http://bb7ea70c-3be24eb08a08b6d39f801985.cloudapp.net,while in the production area you will have a friendly URL like http://aexpense.cloupapp.net. This allows you to test new and updated applications in a private en-vironment that others don't know about. You can also swap the con-tents of the production and staging areas, which makes it easy to roll back the application to the previous version.

◈ *You can quickly roll back a change in production by using the swap operation.*

Note: *The swap is nearly instantaneous because it just involves Windows Azure changing the DNS entries for the two areas.*

For information about rolling upgrades across multiple role instances and partial application upgrades that upgrade individual roles, see the MSDN documentation at http://msdn.microsoft.com/en-us/library/ee517254.aspx.

DEPLOYMENT

To deploy an application to Windows Azure you must upload two files: the service package file that contains all your applications files and the service configuration file that contains your applications configuration data. You can generate the service package file either by using the Cspack.exe utility or by using Visual Studio if you have installed the Windows Azure Tools for Microsoft Visual Studio.

Adatum uses the same package file to deploy to the test and production environments, but they do modify the configuration file. For the aExpense application, the key difference between the contents of the test and production configuration files is the storage connection strings. This information is unique to each Windows Azure subscription and uses randomly generated access keys. Only the two key people in the operations department have access to the storage access keys for the production environment, which makes it impossible for anyone else to use production storage during testing accidentally. Adatum uses a set of scripts to perform the deployment, and one of the tasks of these scripts is to replace the local development storage connection strings in the configuration file with the specific connection strings for the cloud-based storage.

Note: *For more information about the deployment scripts, see Chapter 5, "Phase 2: Automating Deployment and Using Windows Azure Storage."*

TESTING

Adatum tests its cloud-based applications in a number of different environments before it deploys the application to the live production environment.

Developers run unit tests and ad-hoc tests on the development fabric running on their local computers. Although the development fabric is not identical to the cloud environment, it is suitable for developers to run tests on their own code. The build server also runs a suite of tests as a part of the standard build process. This is no different from the normal development practices for on-premises applications.

◈ *Most testing can be performed using the development fabric and development storage.*

You can deploy an application to your Windows Azure test environment just while you run the tests. You only get charged when you use the environment. However, you are charged by the hour, so a 15-minute test will cost the same as a 55-minute test.

The testing team performs the majority of its tests using the local development fabric as well. They only deploy the application to the Windows Azure test environment to test the final configuration of the application before it is passed to the admin team for deployment to production. This way, they can minimize the costs associated with the test environment by limiting the time that they have an application deployed in the cloud.

More Information

MSDN® contains plenty of information about Windows Azure. A good starting to learn more about deploying applications to Windows Azure is at http://msdn.microsoft.com/en-us/library/dd163896.aspx.

The Windows Azure Getting Started page (http://www.microsoft.com/windowsazure/getstarted) contains links to plenty of resources to help you learn about managing applications in Windows Azure.

8

PHASE 4
Adding More Tasks and Tuning the Application

This chapter walks you through the data export feature that Adatum added to the aExpense application, and some of the changes they made following performance testing. The chapter revisits the worker role abstractions introduced in the last phase of the project to illustrate how you can run multiple tasks within a single worker role. It also discusses some architectural issues such as session state management, and the choice of partition and row keys for Windows® Azure™ technology platform table storage.

The Premise

In this phase of the aExpense migration project, the team at Adatum implemented the last key piece of functionality in the application. The aExpense application must generate a file of data that summarizes the approved business expense submissions for a period. Adatum's on-premises payments system imports this data file and then makes the payments to Adatum employees. The current on-premises version of aExpense uses a scheduled SQL Server® Integration Services job to generate the output file and sets the status of an expense submission to "processing" after it is exported. The on-premises application also imports data from the payments processing system to update the status of the expense submissions after the payment processing system makes a payment. This import process is not included in the current phase of the migration project. Figure 1 summarizes the current export process in the on-premises application.

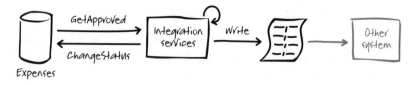

Expenses

FIGURE 1
aExpense export process

Adatum made a number of changes to aExpense following the performance test on the application.

Approved business expense submissions could be anywhere in the table. We want to try to avoid the performance impact that would result from scanning the entire table.

Adatum must automate the process of downloading the expense submission report data for input into the payments processing system.

In this phase, Adatum also evaluated the results from performance testing the application and implemented a number of changes based on those results.

Goals and Requirements

The design of the export process for the cloud version of aExpense must meet a number of goals. First, the costs of the export process should be kept to a minimum while making sure that the export process does not have a negative impact on the performance of the application for users. The export process must also be robust and be able to recover from a failure without compromising the integrity of aExpense's data or the accuracy of the exported data.

The solution must also address the question of how to initiate the export and evaluate whether it should be a manual operation or a scheduled operation. If it is the latter, the team at Adatum must design a mechanism for scheduling tasks in Windows Azure.

The final requirement is to include a mechanism for transferring the data from the cloud-environment to the on-premises environment where the payment processing application can access it.

Overview of the Solution

There are three elements of the export process to consider: how to initiate the process, how to generate the data, and how to download the data from the cloud.

INITIATING THE DATA EXPORT PROCESS

The simplest option for initiating the data export is to have a web page that returns the data on request. There are some potential disadvantages to this approach: First, it adds to the web server's load and potentially affects the other users of the system. In the case of aExpense, this will probably not be significant because the computational requirements for producing the report are low. Second, if the process that generates the data is complex and the data volumes are high, the web page must be able to handle timeouts. Again, for aExpense, it is unlikely that this will be a significant problem. The most significant drawback to this solution in aExpense is that the current storage architecture for expense submission data is optimized for updating and retrieving individual expense submissions by using the user ID. The export process will need to access expense submission data by date and expense state. Unlike SQL Azure where you can define multiple indexes on a table, Windows Azure table storage only has a single index on each table.

Figure 2 illustrates the second option for initiating the data export. Each task has a dedicated worker role, so the image compression and thumbnail generation would be handled by Task 1 in Worker 1, and the data export would be performed by Task 2 in Worker 2. This would also be simple to implement, but in the case of aExpense where the export process will run twice a month, it's not worth the overhead of having a separate role instance. If your task ran more frequently and if it was computationally intensive, you might consider an additional worker role.

Choosing the right PartitionKey and RowKey for your tables is crucial for the performance of your application. Any process that needs a "tablescan" across all your partitions will be slow.

Worker 1

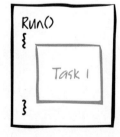

Worker 2

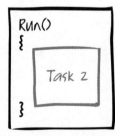

FIGURE 2
Separate worker roles for each task

Figure 3 illustrates the third option where an additional task inside an existing worker role performs the data export process. This approach makes use of existing compute resources and makes sense if the tasks are not too computationally intensive. At the present time, the Windows Azure SDK does not include any task abstractions, so you need to either develop or find a framework to handle task-based processing for you. The team at Adatum will use the "plumbing code" classes described in Chapter 6, "Phase 3: Uploading Images and Adding a Worker Role," to define the tasks in the aExpense application. Designing and building this type of framework is not very difficult, but you do need to include all your own error handling and scheduling logic.

> You should try to use your compute nodes to the full. Remember, you pay for a deployed role instance whether or not it's doing any work. You can also opt for a larger compute instance if you want to do more work in a single role instance.

Worker

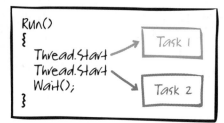

FIGURE 3
Multiple tasks in a single worker role

◈ *Adatum already has some simple abstractions that enable them to run multiple tasks in a single worker role.*

> Windows Azure can only monitor at the level of a worker, and it tries to restart a failed worker if possible. If one of your task processing threads fails, it's up to you to handle the situation.

GENERATING THE EXPORT DATA
The team at Adatum decided to split the expense report generation process into two steps. The first step "flattens" the data model and puts the data into a Windows Azure table. This table uses the expense submission's approval date as the partition key, the expense ID as the row key, and it stores the expense submission total. The second step reads this table and generates a Windows Azure blob that contains the data ready for export as a Comma Separated Values (CSV) file. Adatum implemented each of these two steps as a task by using the "plumbing code" described in Chapter 6, "Phase 3: Uploading Images and Adding a Worker Role." Figure 4 illustrates how the task that adds data to the Windows Azure table works.

First, a manager approves a business expense submission. This updates the status of the submission in table storage, and places a message that contains the expense submission's ID and approval date onto a queue. The task retrieves the message from the queue, calculates the total value of the expense submission from the expense detail items, and stores this as a single line in the Expense Export table. The task also updates the status of the expense submission to be "in process" before it deletes the message from the queue.

Windows Azure table storage does not have all the features of a relational database. You may need multiple tables that present the same data in different ways based on the needs of the application. To make this work, you should be able to generate the derived table in an idempotent way from the data in the original table. Table storage is cheap!

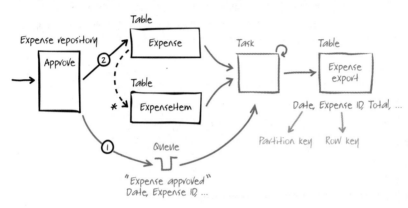

FIGURE 4
Generating the Expense Report table

EXPORTING THE REPORT DATA

To export the data, Adatum considered two options. The first was to have a web page that enables a user to download the expense report data as a file. This page would query the expense report table by date and generate a CSV file that the payments processing system can import. Figure 5 illustrates this option.

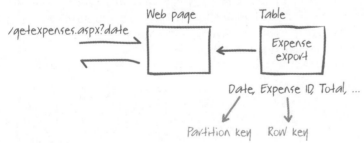

FIGURE 5
Downloading the expense report from a web page

The second option, shown in Figure 6, was to create another job in the worker process that runs on a schedule to generate the file in blob storage ready for download. Adatum will modify the on-premises payment processing system to download this file before importing it. Adatum selected this option because it enables them to schedule the job to run at a quiet time in order to avoid any impact on the performance of the application for users. The on-premises application can access the blob storage directly without involving either the Windows Azure web role or worker role.

> This approach makes it easier for us to automate the download and get the data in time for the payments processing run.

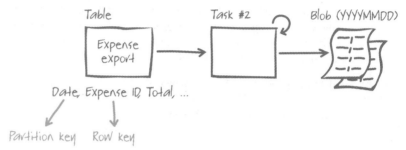

FIGURE 6
Generating the expense report in blob storage

Adatum had to modify slightly the worker role "plumbing code" to support this process. In the original version of the "plumbing code," a message in a queue triggered a task to run, but the application now also requires the ability to schedule tasks.

> We had to modify our "plumbing code" classes slightly to accommodate scheduled tasks.

Inside the Implementation

Now is a good time to walk through these changes in more detail. As you go through this section, you may want to download the Microsoft® Visual Studio® development system solution from http://wag.codeplex.com/. This solution contains the implementation of aExpense after the changes made in this phase. If you are not interested in the mechanics, you should skip to the next section.

GENERATING THE EXPENSE REPORT TABLE

The task that performs this operation uses the worker role "plumbing code" described in Chapter 6, "Phase 3: Uploading Images and Adding a Worker Role." The discussion here will focus on the task implementation and table design issues; it does not focus on the "plumbing code."

This task is the first of two tasks that generate the approved expense data for export. It is responsible for generating the "flattened" table of approved expense data in Windows Azure table storage. The following code sample shows how the expense report export process begins in the **ExpenseRepository** class where the **UpdateApproved** method adds a message to a queue and updates the **Approved** property of the expense header record.

For this task, we were able to use our worker role "plumbing code" without modification.

```
public void UpdateApproved(Expense expense)
{
    var context = new ExpenseDataContext(this.account);

    ExpenseRow expenseRow =
        GetExpenseRowById(context, expense.Id);
    expenseRow.Approved = expense.Approved;

    var queue = new AzureQueueContext(this.account);
    queue.AddMessage(new ApprovedExpenseMessage {
        ExpenseId = expense.Id.ToString(),
        ApproveDate = DateTime.UtcNow });

    context.UpdateObject(expenseRow);
    context.SaveChanges();
}
```

This code uses a new message type named **ApprovedExpense Message** that derives from the "plumbing code" class named **BaseQueueMessage**. The following code sample shows the two properties of the **ApprovedExpenseMessage** class.

```
[DataContract]
public class ApprovedExpenseMessage : BaseQueueMessage
{
    [DataMember]
    public string ExpenseId { get; set; }

    [DataMember]
    public DateTime ApproveDate { get; set; }
}
```

The following code shows how the **ProcessMessage** method in the **ExpenseReportJob** class retrieves the message from the queue and creates a new **ExpenseExport** entity to save to table storage.

> We "flatten" the data and calculate the expense submission total before saving the data into an intermediate table. This table contains the data structured exactly as we need it to do the export.

```csharp
public override bool ProcessMessage(
    ApprovedExpenseMessage message)
{
    try
    {
        Expense expense = this.expenses.GetExpenseById(
            new ExpenseKey(message.ExpenseId));

        if (expense == null)
        {
            return false;
        }

        if (!expense.Approved)
        {
            return true;
        }

        double totalToPay = expense.Details.Sum(x => x.Amount);
        var export = new ExpenseExport
            {
                ApproveDate = message.ApproveDate,
                ApproverName = expense.ApproverName,
                CostCenter = expense.CostCenter,
                ExpenseId = expense.Id,
                ReimbursementMethod = expense.ReimbursementMethod,
                TotalAmount = totalToPay,
                UserName = expense.User.UserName
            };
        this.expenseExports.Save(export);
    }
    catch (InvalidOperationException ex)
    {
        var innerEx =
            ex.InnerException as DataServiceClientException;
```

```
    if (innerEx != null &&
        innerEx.StatusCode == (int)HttpStatusCode.Conflict)
    {
        // The data already exists, so we can return true
        // because we have processed this before.
        return true;
    }
    Log.Write(EventKind.Error, ex.TraceInformation());
    return false;
}

    return true;
}
```

If this method fails for any reason other than a conflict on the insert, the "plumbing code" classes ensure that message is left on the queue. When the **ProcessMessage** method tries to process the message from the queue a second time, the insert to the expense report table fails with a duplicate key error and the inner exception reports this as a conflict in its **StatusCode** property. If this happens, the method can safely return a **true** result.

> We need to ensure that this process is robust. We don't want to lose any expense submissions or pay anyone twice.

If the **Approved** property of the **Expense** object is false, this indicates a failure during the **UpdateApproved** method after it added a message to the queue, but before it updated the table. In this circumstance, the **ProcessMessage** method removes the message from the queue without processing it.

The partition key of the Expense Export table is the expense approval date, and the row key is the expense ID. This optimizes access to this data for queries that use approval date in the **where** clause, which is what the export process requires.

EXPORTING THE DATA

This task is the second of two tasks that generate the approved expense data for export and is responsible for creating a Windows Azure blob that contains a CSV file of approved expense submissions data.

The task that generates the blob containing the expense report data is slightly different from the two other tasks in the aExpense application. The other tasks poll a queue to see if there is any work for them to do. This task is triggered by a schedule, which sets the task to run at fixed times. The team at Adatum had to modify their worker role "plumbing code" classes to support scheduled tasks.

> Choose partition keys and rows keys to optimize your queries against the data. Ideally, you should be able to include the partition key in the **where** block of the query.

◈ *The worker role "plumbing code" classes now support scheduled tasks in addition to tasks that are triggered by a message on a queue.*

You can use the abstract class **JobProcessor**, which implements the **IJobProcessor** interface, to define new scheduled tasks. The following code example shows the **JobProcessor** class.

```
public abstract class JobProcessor : IJobProcessor
{
    private bool keepRunning;

    protected int SleepInterval { get; set; }

    protected JobProcessor(int sleepInterval)
    {
        if (sleepInterval <= 0)
        {
            throw new
                ArgumentOutOfRangeException("sleepInterval");
        }

        this.SleepInterval = sleepInterval;
    }

    public void Run()
    {
        this.keepRunning = true;
        while (this.keepRunning)
        {
            Thread.Sleep(this.SleepInterval);
            this.RunCore();
        }
    }

    public void Stop()
    {
        this.keepRunning = false;
    }

    protected abstract void RunCore();
}
```

> We could extend the application to enable an on-premises application to generate an ad-hoc expense data report by allowing an on-premises application to place a message onto a Windows Azure queue. We could then have a task that generated the report data when it received a message on the queue.

This implementation does not make it easy to specify the exact time that scheduled tasks will run. The time between tasks will be the value of the sleep interval, plus the time taken to run the task. If you need the task to run at fixed time, you should measure how long the task takes to run and subtract that value from the sleep interval.

Note: *The **BaseJobProcessor** class that defines tasks that read messages from queues extends the **JobProcessor** class.*

In the aExpense application, the **ExpenseExportBuilderJob** class extends the **JobProcessor** class to define a scheduled task. The **ExpenseExportBuilderJob** class, shown in the following code example, defines the task that generates the expense report data and stores it as a blob. In this class, the **expenseExports** variable refers to the table of approved expense submissions, and the **exportStorage** variable refers to the report data for downloading in blob storage. The call to the base class constructor specifies the interval at which the job runs. In the **RunCore** method, the code first retrieves all the approved expense submissions from the export table based on the job date. Next, the code appends a CSV record to the export data in the blob storage for each approved expense submission. Finally, the code deletes all the records it copied to the blob storage from the table.

Note: *The following code sets the scheduled interval to a low number for testing and demonstration purposes. You should change this interval for a "real" schedule.*

```
public class ExpenseExportBuilderJob : JobProcessor
{
    private readonly ExpenseExportRepository expenseExports;
    private readonly ExpenseExportStorage exportStorage;

    public ExpenseExportBuilderJob() : base(100000)
    {
        this.expenseExports = new ExpenseExportRepository();
        this.exportStorage = new ExpenseExportStorage();
    }

    protected override void RunCore()
    {
        DateTime jobDate = DateTime.UtcNow;
        string name = jobDate.ToExpenseExportKey();

        IEnumerable<ExpenseExport> exports =
            this.expenseExports.Retreive(jobDate);
        if (exports == null || exports.Count() == 0)
        {
            return;
        }

        string text = this.exportStorage.GetExport(name);
```

```
        var exportText = new StringBuilder(text);
        foreach (ExpenseExport expenseExport in exports)
        {
            exportText.AppendLine(expenseExport.ToCsvLine());
        }

        this.exportStorage.AddExport(name,
            exportText.ToString(), "text/plain");

        // Delete the exports.
        foreach (ExpenseExport exportToDelete in exports)
        {
            try
            {
                this.expenseExports.Delete(exportToDelete);
            }
            catch (InvalidOperationException ex)
            {
                Log.Write(EventKind.Error,
                    ex.TraceInformation());
            }
        }
    }
}
```

If the process fails before it deletes all the approved expense submissions from the export table, any undeleted approved expense submissions will be exported a second time when the task next runs. However, the exported CSV data includes the expense ID and the approval date of the expense submission, so the on-premises payment processing system will be able to identify duplicate items.

The following code shows the queries that the **RunCore** method invokes to retrieve approved expense submissions and deletes them after it copies them to the export blob. Because they use the job date to identify the partitions to search, these queries are fast and efficient.

```
public IEnumerable<ExpenseExport> Retreive(DateTime jobDate)
{
    var context = new ExpenseDataContext(this.account);
    string compareDate = jobDate.ToExpenseExportKey();
    var query = (from export in context.ExpenseExport
            where export.PartitionKey.CompareTo(compareDate) <= 0
            select export).AsTableServiceQuery();
```

```
    var val = query.Execute();
    return val.Select(e => e.ToModel()).ToList();
}

public void Delete(ExpenseExport expenseExport)
{
    var context = new ExpenseDataContext(this.account);
    var query = (from export in context.ExpenseExport
      where export.PartitionKey.CompareTo(
        expenseExport.ApproveDate.ToExpenseExportKey()) == 0 &&
        export.RowKey.CompareTo(
        expenseExport.ExpenseId.ToString()) == 0
      select export).AsTableServiceQuery();
    ExpenseExportRow row = query.Execute().SingleOrDefault();
    if (row == null)
    {
        return;
    }

    context.DeleteObject(row);
    context.SaveChanges();
}
```

Performance Testing, Tuning, To-Do Items

As part of the work for this phase, the team at Adatum evaluated the results from performance testing the application, and as a result, it made a number of changes to the aExpense application. They also documented some of the key "missing" pieces in the application that Adatum should address in the next phase of the project.

Adatum made changes to the aExpense application following their performance testing.

STORING SESSION STATE

In preparation for performance testing, and to ensure the scalability of the application, the team at Adatum made some changes to the way that the application handles session state. The AddExpense.aspx page uses session state to maintain a list of expense items before the user saves the completed business expense submission. During development and testing, the application used the default, in-memory, session state provider. This default in-memory session state provider is not suitable for scenarios with multiple web role instances, because the session state is not synchronized between instances, and the Windows Azure load balancer could route a request to any available instance. Adatum evaluated several approaches to resolve this issue in the aExpense application.

If your application has to scale to more than one web role, any session state must be shared across the worker role instances.

The first option considered was to use ASP.NET view state instead of session state so that the application maintains its state data on the client. This solution would work when the application has multiple web role instances because the application does not store any state data on the server. Because the aExpense application stores scanned images in the state before the application saves the whole expense submission, this means that the state can be quite large. Using view state would be a poor solution in this case because it would need to move the data in the view state over the network, using up bandwidth and adversely affecting the application's performance.

> Using ASP.NET view state is an excellent solution as long as the amount of data involved is small. This is not the case with the aExpense application where the state data includes images.

The second option is to continue to use session state but use a provider that persists the state to server-side storage that is accessible from multiple web role instances. In Windows Azure, the server side storage could be either SQL Azure or table and blob storage. SQL Azure storage is relatively expensive, compared to table and blob storage, so Adatum decided to use a session state provider for Windows Azure table and blob storage. The solution uses a sample provider that you can download from http://code.msdn.microsoft.com/windowsazuresamples. The only change required for the application to use a different session state provider is in the Web.config file.

> **Note:** *The **TableStorageSessionStateProvider** class is unsupported code and currently does not include any tidy up routines. If you use this provider, you must develop a mechanism to remove expired sessions from storage. Adatum plans to add an additional job to the aExpense worker role to perform this task. You can find the **TableStorageSessionStateProvider** class in the Providers folder of the aExpense project in the solution.*

> You must ensure that you have some way of removing expired sessions from storage. The aExpense application could have an additional job in its worker role to perform this task.

TOO MANY CALLS TO THE CREATEIFNOTEXIST METHOD

Originally, the constructor for the **ExpenseReceiptStorage** class was responsible for checking that the expense receipt container existed, and creating it if necessary. This constructor is invoked whenever the application instantiates an **ExpenseRepository** object or a **ReceiptThumbnailJob** object. The **CreateIfNotExist** method that checks whether a container exists requires a round-trip to the storage server and incurs a storage transaction cost. To avoid these unnecessary round-trips, Adatum moved this logic to the **Initialize** method in the **WebRole** class.

PREVENTING USERS FROM UPLOADING LARGE IMAGES

To prevent users from uploading large images of receipt scans to aExpense, Adatum configured the application to allow a maximum upload size of 1,024 kilobytes (KB) to the AddExpense.aspx page. The following code example shows the setting in the Web.config file.

```
<location path="AddExpense.aspx">
  <system.web>
    <authorization>
      <allow roles="Employee" />
      <deny users="*"/>
    </authorization>
    <httpRuntime maxRequestLength="1024"/>
  </system.web>
</location>
```

VALIDATING USER INPUT

The cloud-based version of aExpense does not perform comprehensive checks on user input for invalid or dangerous items. The AddExpense.aspx file includes some basic validation that checks the length of user input, but Adatum should add additional validation checks to the **OnAddNewExpenseItemClick** method in the AddExpense.aspx.cs file.

PAGING AND SORTING ON THE DEFAULT.ASPX PAGE

During performance testing, the response times on Default.aspx degraded as the test script added more and more expense submissions for a user. This happened because the current version of the Default.aspx page does not include any paging mechanism, so it always displays all the expense submissions for a user. As a temporary measure, Adatum modified the LINQ query that retrieves expense submissions by user to include a **Take(10)** clause, so that the application only requests the first 10 expense submissions. In a future phase of the project, Adatum will add paging functionality to the Default.aspx page.

> **Note:** For a discussion about how Adatum might implement paging on the Default.aspx and Approve.aspx, see the section "Implementing Paging with Windows Azure Table Storage" below.

Adatum also realized that their original choice of a GUID as the row key for the expense table was not optimal. The default ordering of expense submissions should be in reverse chronological order, because most users will want to see their most recent expense submissions at the top of the list or on the first page when Adatum implements paging. The expense approval page will also use this ordering.

To implement this change, Adatum modified the **Expense** class in the **AExpense.Model** namespace by changing the type of the **Id** property from **Guid** to **ExpenseKey**. The following code example shows how the static **Now** property of the **ExpenseKey** class generates an inverted tick count to use in its **InvertedTicks** property.

```
public static ExpenseKey Now
{
    get
    {
        return new ExpenseKey(
            string.Format("{0:D19}",
            DateTime.MaxValue.Ticks - DateTime.UtcNow.Ticks));
    }
}
```

The query that retrieves expense submissions by user now returns them in reverse chronological order.

SYSTEM.NET CONFIGURATION CHANGES

The following code example shows two configuration changes that Adatum made to the aExpense application to improve its performance.

```
<system.net>
  <settings>
    <servicePointManager expect100Continue="false" />
  </settings>
  <connectionManagement>
    <add address = "*" maxconnection = "24" />
  </connectionManagement>
</system.net>
```

The first change switches off the "Expect 100-continue" feature. If this feature is enabled, when the application sends a PUT or POST request, it can delay sending the payload by sending an "Expect 100-continue" header. When the server receives this message, it uses the available information in the header to check whether it could make the call, and if it can, it sends back a status code 100 to the client. The client then sends the remainder of the payload. This means that the client can check for many common errors without sending the payload. If you have tested the client well enough to ensure that it is not sending any bad requests, you can turn off the "Expect 100-continue" feature and reduce the number of round trips to the server. This is especially useful when the client sends many messages with small payloads, for example, when the client is using the table or queue service.

The second configuration change increases the maximum number of connections that the web server will maintain from its default value of **2**. If this value is set too low, the problem manifests itself through "Underlying connection was closed" messages.

> **Note:** *The exact number to use for this setting depends on your application. The page at http://support.microsoft.com/kb/821268 has useful information about how to set this for server side applications. You can also set it for a particular URI by specifying the URI in place of "*".*

We made a number of changes to our WCF Data Services code to improve performance.

WCF DATA SERVICE OPTIMIZATIONS

Because of a known performance issue with WCF Data Services, Adatum defined a **ResolveType** delegate on the **DataServiceContext** class in the aExpense application. Without this delegate, query performance degrades as the number of entities that the query returns increases. The following code example shows the delegate definition.

```
private static Type ResolveEntityType(string name)
{
    var tableName = name.Split(new[] { '.' }).Last();
    switch (tableName)
    {
        case ExpenseTable:
            return typeof(ExpenseRow);
        case ExpenseItemTable:
            return typeof(ExpenseItemRow);
        case ExpenseExportTable:
            return typeof(ExpenseExportRow);
    }

    throw new ArgumentException(
        string.Format(
            CultureInfo.InvariantCulture,
            "Could not resolve the table name '{0}'
            to a known entity type.", name));
}
```

> **Note:** *Instead of using the **ResolveType** delegate, you can avoid the performance problem by ensuring that your entity class names exactly match the table names.*

Adatum added a further optimization to the WCF Data Services client code by setting the **MergeOption** to **NoTracking** for the queries in the **ExpenseRepository** class. If you are not making any changes to the entities that WCF Data Services retrieve, there is no need for the **DataContext** object to initialize change tracking for entities.

Implementing Paging with Windows Azure Table Storage

Adatum have not implemented any paging functionality in the current phase of the project, but this section gives an outline of the approach they intend to take. The **ResultSegment** class in the Windows Azure StorageClient library provides an opaque **ContinuationToken** property that you can use to access the next set of results from a query if that query did not return the full set of results, for example, if the query used the **Take** operator to return a small number of results to display on a page. This **ContinuationToken** property will form the basis of any paging implementation.

The **ResultSegment** class only returns a **ContinuationToken** object to access the next page of results, and not the previous page, so if your application requires the ability to page backward, you must store **ContinuationToken** objects that point to previous pages. A stack is a suitable data structure to use. Figure 7 shows the state of a stack after a user has browsed to the first page and then paged forward as far as the third page.

By implementing paging, we can improve the performance of the application by returning just the data the user needs to see.

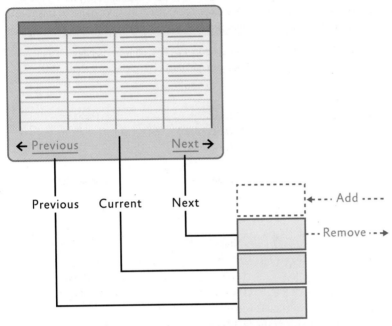

FIGURE 7
Displaying page 3 of the data from a table

If a user clicks the **Next** hyperlink to browse to page 4, the page peeks at the stack to get the continuation token for page 4. After the page executes the query with the continuation token from the stack, it pushes a new continuation token for page 5 onto the stack.

If a user clicks the **Previous** hyperlink to browse to page 2, the page will pop two entries from the stack, and then peek at the stack to get the continuation token for page 2. After the page executes the query with the continuation token from the stack, it will push a new continuation for page 3 onto the stack.

The following code examples show how Adatum could implement this behavior on an asynchronous ASP.NET page.

Note: *Using an asynchronous page frees up the pages thread from the thread pool while a potentially long-running I/O operation takes place. This improves throughput on the web server and increases the scalability of the application.*

The following two code examples show how to create an asynchronous ASP.NET page. First, add an **Async="true"** attribute to the page directive in the .aspx file.

```
<%@ Page Language="C#" AutoEventWireup="true"
CodeBehind="Default.aspx.cs" Inherits="ContinuationSpike._De-
fault" Async="true"%>
```

Second, register begin and end methods for the asynchronous operation in the load event for the page.

```
protected void Page_Load(object sender, EventArgs e)
{

    AddOnPreRenderCompleteAsync(
        new BeginEventHandler(BeginAsyncOperation),
        new EndEventHandler(EndAsyncOperation)
    );
}
```

We need to store the stack containing the continuation tokens as a part of the session state.

The following code example shows the definition of the **Continuation Stack** class that the application uses to store continuation tokens in the session state.

```
public class ContinuationStack
{
    private readonly Stack stack;

    public ContinuationStack()
    {
        this.stack = new Stack();
    }
```

```csharp
    public bool CanMoveBack()
    {
        if (this.stack.Count >= 2)
            return true;

        return false;
    }

    public bool CanMoveForward()
    {
        return this.GetForwardToken() != null;
    }

    public ResultContinuation GetBackToken()
    {
        if (this.stack.Count == 0)
            return null;
        // Need to pop twice and then return what is left.
        this.stack.Pop();
        this.stack.Pop();
        if (this.stack.Count == 0)
            return null;
        return this.stack.Peek() as ResultContinuation;
    }

    public ResultContinuation GetForwardToken()
    {
        if (this.stack.Count == 0)
            return null;

        return this.stack.Peek() as ResultContinuation;
    }

    public void AddToken(ResultContinuation result)
    {
        this.stack.Push(result);
    }
}
```

The following code example shows the **BeginAsyncOperation** method that starts the query execution for the next page of data. The **ct** value in the query string specifies the direction to move.

```csharp
private IAsyncResult BeginAsyncOperation(object sender, EventArgs
e, AsyncCallback cb, object extradata)
{
    var query =
      new MessageContext(CloudConfiguration.GetStorageAccount())
      .Messages.Take(3).AsTableServiceQuery();
    if (Request["ct"] == "forward")
    {
        var segment = this.ContinuationStack.GetForwardToken();
        return query.BeginExecuteSegmented(segment, cb, query);
    }

    if (Request["ct"] == "back")
    {
        var segment = this.ContinuationStack.GetBackToken();
        return query.BeginExecuteSegmented(segment, cb, query);
    }
    return query.BeginExecuteSegmented(cb, query);
}
```

The **EndAsyncOperation** method puts the query results into the messages list and pushes the new continuation token onto the stack.

```csharp
private List<MessageEntity> messages;

private void EndAsyncOperation(IAsyncResult result)
{
    var cloudTableQuery =
        result.AsyncState as CloudTableQuery<MessageEntity>;
    ResultSegment<MessageEntity> resultSegment =
        cloudTableQuery.EndExecuteSegmented(result);
    this.ContinuationStack.AddToken(
        resultSegment.ContinuationToken);
    this.messages = resultSegment.Results.ToList();
}
```

More Information

A useful site for guidance on performance optimizations for your Windows Azure applications is AzureScope at http://azurescope.cloudapp.net/Default.aspx.

You can read detailed guidance on using Windows Azure table storage in this document: http://go.microsoft.com/fwlink/?LinkId=153401.

You can read detailed guidance on using Windows Azure blob storage in this document: http://go.microsoft.com/fwlink/?LinkId=153400.

Appendix A

Creating a Cloud Project in Visual Studio

This appendix shows how to create a new cloud project in Microsoft® Visual Studio® development system by using the Windows® Azure™ Cloud Service template. All the scenarios in this book were created by using this template.

The best way to install the template in your copy of Visual Studio is to download and install the Windows Azure Tools for Microsoft Visual Studio, which includes the Windows Azure SDK. You can find the latest version of this installer by searching on the Microsoft Download Center (http://www.microsoft.com/downloads).

Creating a New Cloud Project in Visual Studio

This procedure shows how to create a Visual Studio solution that contains the projects that you need to start creating a cloud application.

To create a new Windows Azure Cloud Service project

1. In Visual Studio, in the **New Project** dialog box, in **Project types**, expand either **Visual C#** or **Visual Basic**, and then click **Cloud**.

2. In **Templates**, click **Windows Azure Cloud Service**. Enter suitable values for **Name**, **Location**, and **Solution Name**, and then click **OK**.

3. In the **New Cloud Service Project** dialog box, add the roles that you need to the **Cloud Service Solution** list.

4. Rename the roles in the **Cloud Service Solution** list with meaningful names, and then click **OK**.

Note: *You can add multiple roles of the same type. For example, your application could have one ASP.NET web role and two worker roles. You can also add roles to your solution later by right-clicking the cloud project in Solution Explorer.*

Understanding the Projects in the Solution

If, in the preceding procedure, you created one web role and one worker role, you will find three projects in your solution:

- There will be one cloud project that contains the Service-Configuration.cscfg file, the ServiceDefinition.csdef file, and a folder named Roles.
- There will be one project for the web role. This project looks like a standard ASP.NET project with an additional file named WebRole.cs or WebRole.vb.
- There will be one project for the worker role. This project contains a file named WorkerRole.cs or WorkerRole.vb.

THE CLOUD SERVICE PROJECT

The ServiceConfiguration.cscfg and ServiceDefinition.csdef files are XML files that contain the configuration data that tells Windows Azure how to deploy and run the application. Although you can manually edit the XML, you can also edit the configuration data by right-clicking on a role in the **Roles** folder and selecting **Properties**.

Configuration options for a role include the following:

- The .NET trust level
- The number of instances of the role to run in the service
- The size of the virtual machine in to which you want to deploy role instances
- The connection string for accessing storage for diagnostic data

Configuration options for a web role also include the following:

- Endpoint definitions
- Certificates required for HTTPS endpoints

THE WEB ROLE PROJECT

A web role project is based on a standard ASP.NET project. The Web.config file includes the configuration settings for the Windows Azure trace listener. The WebRole.cs or WebRole.vb file enables you to override the role's life cycle methods (**OnStart**, **OnStop**, and **Run**) of the role.

THE WORKER ROLE PROJECT

In a worker role project, the App.config file contains configuration settings for the Windows Azure trace listener. The WorkerRole.cs or WorkerRole.vb file enables you to override the role's life cycle methods (**OnStart**, **OnStop**, and **Run**) of the role.

Appendix B   Using the Windows Azure Service Management API

The Windows Azure Service Management API is a REST-based API that enables you to manage your Windows Azure deployments, hosted services, and storage accounts. You can create your own client-side utilities that use this API or use an existing utility like **csmanage** at http://code.msdn.microsoft.com/windowsazuresamples or the Windows Azure Service Management CmdLets at http://code.msdn.microsoft.com/azurecmdlets.

The Windows Azure Service Management API currently includes the following storage account operations:

- List storage accounts.
- Get storage account properties.
- Get storage account keys.
- Regenerate storage account keys.

The Windows Azure Service Management API currently includes the following hosted service operations:

- List hosted services.
- Get hosted service properties.
- Create, get, swap, delete, and upgrade deployment.
- Change deployment configuration.
- Update deployment status.
- Walk upgrade domain.

The Windows Azure Service Management API currently includes the following certificate operations:

- List, get, add, and delete certificates.

The Windows Azure Service Management API currently includes the following affinity group operations:

- List and get affinity groups.

There are some operations that you cannot perform using the Windows Azure Service Management API and that you can only perform manually through the Windows Azure Developer Portal:

- Create and delete affinity groups.
- Create and delete storage accounts.

- Create and delete hosted services.
- Update the labels of affinity groups, hosted services, and storage accounts.
- Register and unregister a storage account with Content Delivery Network (CDN) and associate a CNAME with it.
- Register and unregister a custom domain name with a storage account.

The Windows Azure Service Management API uses a certificate to authenticate calls from a client. To use the API, you first need to obtain an X.509 certificate with a key size of at least 2,048 bits. You can use Internet Information Services (IIS) 7 to generate a self-signed certificate or use the **makecert** tool that is available as part of the Windows SDK (http://go.microsoft.com/fwlink/?linkid=84091). To generate a suitable certificate with **makecert**, use the following command.

```
makecert -r -pe -a sha1 -n "CN=Windows Azure Authentication
Certificate" -ss My -len 2048 -sp "Microsoft Enhanced RSA and AES
Cryptographic Provider" -sy 24 testcert.cer
```

For more help with using the **makecert** utility, see the page at http://msdn.microsoft.com/en-us/library/bfsktky3(VS.90).aspx.

You must then upload the .cer file to the Windows Azure Developer Portal by using the **Manage My API Certificates** link on the Account page.

When you use any of the operations in the Windows Azure Service Management API, you must include the certificate in the equest.

Appendix C   Using the Windows Azure Service Management CmdLets in a 64-bit Environment

If you are running a 64-bit version of Windows and you want to be able to invoke a PowerShell script that uses the Windows Azure Service CmdLets from an MSBuild task, you must use the 32-bit version of PowerShell. This is because the targets file that MSBuild uses for Windows Azure is in the x86 Program Files folder.

To build 32-bit versions of the Windows Azure Service Management CmdLets on a 64-bit computer, create the following batch files in the setup\dependency_checker\scripts\tasks folder under the folder where you installed the Windows Azure Service Management Cmdlets.

```
build-x86.cmd
@echo off
@REM -----------------------------------------------------------
---------------------
@REM Build Azure Services Management Tools Solution
@REM -----------------------------------------------------------
---------------------

set verbosity=quiet
set pause=true

:: Check for 64-bit Framework
REM if exist %SystemRoot%\Microsoft.NET\Framework64\v3.5 (
REM  set msbuild=%SystemRoot%\Microsoft.NET\Framework64\v3.5\
msbuild.exe
REM  goto :run
REM )
:: Check for 32-bit Framework
if exist %SystemRoot%\Microsoft.NET\Framework\v3.5 (
  set msbuild=%SystemRoot%\Microsoft.NET\Framework\v3.5\msbuild.
exe
```

```
  goto :run
)

@echo Building "AzureManagementTools.Cmdlets.csproj"
:run
call %msbuild% "..\..\..\..\code\AzureManagementTools.Cmdlets\
AzureManagementTools.Cmdlets.csproj" /t:ReBuild /
verbosity:%verbosity%

@if errorlevel 1 goto :error
@echo Build Complete

@goto :exit

:error
@echo An Error Occured building the Azure Services Management
Tools Solution

:exit
```

installPSSnapIn-x86.cmd
```
@echo off
%~d0
cd "%~dp0"

ECHO ----------------------------------------
ECHO Installing AzureManagementTools PSSnapIn
ECHO ----------------------------------------

ECHO "Build solution..."
call .\build-x86.cmd

REM IF EXIST %WINDIR%\SysWow64 (
REM     set installUtilDir=%WINDIR%\Microsoft.NET\Framework64\
v2.0.50727
REM ) ELSE (
        set installUtilDir=%WINDIR%\Microsoft.NET\Framework\
v2.0.50727
REM )

set assemblyPath="..\..\..\..\code\AzureManagementTools.Cmdlets\
bin\Debug\Microsoft.Samples.AzureManagementTools.PowerShell.dll"

ECHO "Installing PSSnapIn..."
```

```
%installUtilDir%\installutil.exe -i %assemblyPath%

@PAUSE
```

uninstallPSSnapIn-x86.cmd
```
@echo off
%~d0
cd "%~dp0"

ECHO ----------------------------------------
ECHO Uninstall AzureManagementTools PSSnapIn
ECHO ----------------------------------------

REM IF EXIST %WINDIR%\SysWow64 (
REM     set installUtilDir=%WINDIR%\Microsoft.NET\Framework64\
v2.0.50727
REM ) ELSE (
        set installUtilDir=%WINDIR%\Microsoft.NET\Framework\
v2.0.50727
REM )

set assemblyPath="..\..\..\..\code\AzureManagementTools.Cmdlets\
bin\Debug\Microsoft.Samples.AzureManagementTools.PowerShell.dll"

ECHO "Uninstalling PSSnapIn..."
%installUtilDir%\installutil.exe -u %assemblyPath%

@PAUSE
```

Then run installPSSnapIn-x86.cmd from a command prompt to install the CmdLets. To uninstall the CmdLets, run unistallPSSnapIn-x86. cmd.

Appendix D

Using DNS with Windows Azure

When you deploy your application to Windows Azure and move it to the production environment, Windows Azure provides a friendly DNS name so can access your application at a URL like http://aexpense.cloudapp.net. However, you will probably want to use your own custom URL like https://aexpense.adatumapps.com. You'll also notice that if you want to use HTTPS, you must install a certificate that matches the custom DNS name in your hosted service.

> **Note:** *You cannot get a valid certificate for Cloudapp.net.*

The deployment script for the aExpense application demonstrates how to install a certificate for your Windows Azure application.

To map a domain name to an address, you have two options.

1. You can map the A record to a specific IP address.

2. You can use a CNAME record to map a subdomain to another DNS entry.

The first option is not suitable for a Windows Azure application because Windows Azure reserves the right to change the IP address that Windows Azure assigns to your application.

The second option works well with Windows Azure. Using the tools provided by your domain registrar, you must map the subdomain you want to use for your application to the name provided by Windows Azure. For example, if your application has the domain name aexpense.cloudapp.net in Windows Azure and you have registered the domain name adatumapps.com, you could create a CNAME entry that maps the www subdomain to aexpense.cloudapp.net making your application accessible using the name www.adatumapps.com. Another option would be to use a CNAME entry to map the aexpense subdomain to aexpense.cloudapp.net making your application accessible using the name aexpense.adatumapps.com. This approach will continue to work if Windows Azure assigns a new IP address to your application.

If you plan to make your application unavailable at certain times, you can modify the CNAME entry to point to a static HTML page on your own servers at those times. The static HTML page can inform users that the application is unavailable.

Appendix E   Windows Azure Storage Management Tools

There are a number of scenarios where it is useful to have the ability to manage your Windows Azure storage accounts remotely. For example, during development and testing, you might want to be able to examine the contents of your tables, queues, and blobs to verify that your application is behaving as expected. You may also need to insert test data directly into your storage. In a production environment, you may need to examine the contents of your application's storage during troubleshooting or view diagnostic data that you have persisted. You may also want to download your diagnostic data for offline analysis and to be able to delete stored log files to reduce your storage costs.

A web search will reveal a growing number of third-party tools that can fulfill these roles. This appendix describes two simple tools to get you started.

Windows Azure Management Tool (MMC)

This MMC snap-in is available at http://code.msdn.microsoft.com/windowsazuremmc. Using this tool, you can define connections for managing multiple storage accounts, including local development storage. The snap-in includes the following features:

- For blob storage, you can create containers, delete containers, and manage container permissions. You can also upload, download, and delete blobs. There is also a useful feature that enables you to upload and download containers as folders.
- For queue storage, the snap-in enables you to view the contents of queues, create new queues, and delete queues. You can also add messages to queues and purge queues.

The current version of this tool does not support Windows Azure table storage.

Windows Azure Storage Explorer

This stand-alone graphical user interface (GUI) tool is available at http://azurestorageexplorer.codeplex.com/. Using this tool, you can define connections for managing multiple storage accounts, including local development storage. The utility includes the following features:

- For blob storage, you can create containers, delete containers, and manage container permissions. You can upload, download, and delete individual blobs. You can also preview some data types and edit text blobs.
- For queue storage, the utility enables you to view the contents of a queue, create new queues, and delete queues. You can also add messages to queues, pop messages off queues, preview messages, and purge queues.
- For table storage, you can use the utility to browse the contents of tables, create, delete, and empty tables. You can also upload and download tables as comma-separated value (CSV) data.

Appendix F

Creating a Self-Signed Certificate for Testing

To test your application using an HTTPS endpoint, you need a suitable test certificate. You can easily generate a certificate by using Internet Information Services (IIS) 7.

To create a self-signed certificate to use with SSL

1. From Administrative Tools in Control Panel, start the **Internet Information Services (IIS) Manager** console.

2. On the home page, double-click **Server Certificates**, and then in the Actions pane, click **Create Self-Signed Certificate**.

3. In the Create Self-Signed Certificate wizard, on the Specify Friendly Name page, type in a name for your certificate, and then click **OK**.

To export the key to a .pfx file that you can upload to Windows Azure

1. In the **Server Certificates** list in the Internet Information Services (IIS) Manager console, select the certificate that you created in the previous procedure.

2. In the Actions pane, click **Export**, select a name and location to save the .pfx file, and then enter a password. You will need this password when you upload the certificate to Windows Azure.

3. Click **OK** to export and save the .pfx file.

Glossary

affinity group. A named grouping that is in a single data center. It can include all the components associated with an application, such as storage, SQL Azure databases, and roles.

claim. A statement about a subject; for example, a name, identity, key, group, permission, or capability made by one subject about itself or another subject. Claims are given one or more values and then packaged in security tokens that are distributed by the issuer.

cloud. A set of interconnected servers located in one or more data centers.

code near. When an application and its associated database(s) are both in the cloud.

code far. When an application is on-premises and its associated database(s) are in the cloud.

content delivery network (CDN). A system composed of multiple servers that contain copies of data. These servers are located in different geographical areas so that users can access the copy that is closes to them.

development fabric. Simulates the Windows® AzureTM fabric so that you can run and test a service locally before deploying it.

Enterprise Library. A collection of reusable software components (application blocks) designed to assist software developers with common enterprise development cross-cutting concerns (such as logging, validation, data access, exception handling, and many others).

horizontal scalability. The ability to add more servers that are copies of existing servers.

hosted service. Spaces where applications are deployed.

idempotent operation. An operation that can be performed multiple times without changing the result. An example is setting a variable.

lease. An exclusive write lock on a blob that lasts until the lease expires.

optimistic concurrency. A concurrency control method that assumes that multiple changes to data can complete without affecting each other; therefore, there is no need to lock the data resources. Optimistic concurrency assumes that concurrency violations occur infrequently and simply disallows any updates or deletions that cause a concurrency violation.

poison message. A message that contains malformed data that causes the queue processor to throw an exception. The result is that the message isn't processed, stays in the queue, and the next attempt to process it once again fails.

Representational State Transfer (REST). An architectural style for retrieving information from Web sites. A resource is the source of specific information. Each resource is identified by a global identifier, such as a Uniform Resource Identifier (URI) in HTTP. The representation is the actual document that conveys the information.

SQL Azure. A relational database management system (RDBMS) in the cloud. SQL Azure is independent of the storage that is a part of Windows Azure. It is based on SQL Server® and can store structured, semi-structured, and unstructured data.

service configuration file. Sets values for the service that can be configured while the service is running in the fabric. The values you can specify in the service configuration file include the number of instances that you want to deploy for each role, the values for the configuration parameters that you established in the service definition file, and the thumbprints for any SSL certificates associated with the service.

service definition file. Defines the roles that comprise a service, optional local storage resources, configuration settings, and certificates for SSL endpoints.

service package. Packages the role binaries and service definition file for publication to the Windows Azure fabric.

snapshot. A read-only copy of a blob.

vertical scalability. The ability to increase a computer's resources, such as memory or CPUs.

Web role. An interactive application that runs in the cloud. A web role can be implemented with any technology that works with Internet Information Services (IIS) 7.

Windows Azure. Microsoft's platform for cloud-based computing. It is provided as a service over the Internet. It includes a computing environment, Windows Azure storage, management services, and the AppFabric.

Windows Azure AppFabric. Provides cloud services for connecting applications running in the cloud or on premises as well as access control services. Not to be confused with the Windows Azure fabric.

Windows Azure fabric. Provides physical machines for compute and storage.

Windows Azure storage. Consists of blobs, tables, and queues. It is accessible with HTTP/HTTPS requests. It is distinct from SQL Azure.

worker role. Performs batch processes and background tasks. Worker roles can make outbound calls and open endpoints for incoming calls. Worker roles typically use queues to communicate with Web roles.

Index

More Resources for Developers

Microsoft Press® books

VISUAL STUDIO

Inside the Microsoft® Build Engine: Using MSBuild and Team Foundation Build
Sayed Ibrahim Hashimi,
William Bartholomew
978-07356-2628-7

Microsoft .NET: Architecting Applications for the Enterprise
Dino Esposito,
Andrea Saltarello
978-07356-2609-6

Microsoft .NET and SAP
Juergen Daiberl, et al.
978-07356-2568-6

**Microsoft Visual Basic® 2008 Express Edition:
Build a Program Now!**
Patrice Pelland
978-07356-2541-9

Microsoft Visual Basic 2008
Step by Step
Michael Halvorson
978-07356-2537-2

Microsoft Visual C#® 2008
Step by Step
John Sharp
978-07356-2430-6

Programming Microsoft Visual C# 2008: The Language
Donis Marshall
978-07356-2540-2

Microsoft Visual Studio® Tips
Sara Ford
978-07356-2640-9

**Windows® via C/C++,
Fifth Edition**
Jeffrey Richter,
Christophe Nasarre
978-07356-2424-5

**Microsoft XNA® Game Studio 3.0:
Learn Programming Now!**
Rob Miles
978-07356-2658-4

WEB DEVELOPMENT

Developing Service-Oriented AJAX Applications on the Microsoft Platform
Daniel Larson
978-07356-2591-4

Introducing Microsoft Silverlight™ 3
Laurence Moroney
978-07356-2573-0

JavaScript
Step by Step
Steve Suehring
978-07356-2449-8

Microsoft ASP.NET and AJAX: Architecting Web Applications
Dino Esposito
978-07356-2621-8

Microsoft ASP.NET 3.5
Step by Step
George Shepherd
978-07356-2426-9

Programming Microsoft ASP.NET 3.5
Dino Esposito
978-07356-2527-3

Microsoft Visual Web Developer™ 2008 Express Edition
Step by Step
Eric Griffin
978-07356-2606-5

.NET FRAMEWORK

**CLR via C#,
Second Edition**
Jeffrey Richter
978-07356-2163-3

3D Programming for Windows
Charles Petzold
978-07356-2394-1

DATA ACCESS/ DATABASE

**Microsoft SQL Server®
2008 Internals**
Kalen Delaney, et al.
978-07356-2624-9

Inside Microsoft SQL Server 2008: T-SQL Querying
Itzik Ben-Gan, et al.
978-07356-2603-4

Programming Microsoft SQL Server 2008
Leonard Lobel, Andrew J. Brust, Stephen Forte
978-07356-2599-0

Smart Business Intelligence Solutions with Microsoft SQL Server 2008
Lynn Langit, et al.
978-07356-2580-8

OTHER TOPICS

Agile Portfolio Management
Jochen Krebs
978-07356-2567-9

Agile Project Management with Scrum
Ken Schwaber
978-07356-1993-7

How We Test Software at Microsoft
Alan Page, Ken Johnston,
Bj Rollison
978-07356-2425-2

Practical Project Initiation
Karl E. Wiegers
978-07356-2521-1

Simple Architectures for Complex Enterprises
Roger Sessions
978-07356-2578-5

Software Estimation: Demystifying the Black Art
Steve McConnell
978-0-7356-0535-0